THE INSIDER'S
GUIDE TO
SEDONA

THE INSIDER'S GUIDE TO SEDONA

by Dennis Andres

MetaAdventures
Sedona, Arizona

Dedicated to the Insiders:
Thanks for all your efforts.
You will always be appreciated.
D.G., T.C., T.S., L.B²., J.F., A.F.,
L.B., M.N., P.C., J.C., D.T., M.N.,
N.A., S.B., L.L., K.B.

ISBN 0-9721202-1-1

Printed in Canada

META ADVENTURES

583 Circle Drive

Sedona, Arizona 86336

Tel. 928.204.2201

e-mail dennis@sedona.net

www.metaadventures.com

For the latest updates on everything you need to know about Sedona,
visit www.SedonaInsider.com

Cover photographs: Larry Lindahl
Interior photographs: Dennis Andres
Design, production, and editorial consultation: Carol Haralson Design
Copyediting: Patricia Barnum

a to z

Inside the Insider's Guide to Sedona

ESSAYS: Insider Insights

MAPS

ENTERING
SEDONA
ELEVATION 4500
FOUNDED 1902
AN ARIZONA MAIN STREET CITY

INTRODUCTION

N O MATTER WHERE YOU GO around the world, it always helps to have a friend to greet you. My life has been a happy example of this truth. From Asia to Africa, South America to Europe, people all over the world have taken what was theirs and shared it freely with me. From Central Asia to the Canadian Rockies, I have been sheltered and guided by generous, hospitable human beings. Knowing I'd be safely taken care of, I could feel free to roam. With local friends to guide my way, I could laugh lightly and explore deeply.

Each year, thousands of visitors wander Red Rock Country with no such friend. Stuck with only the guidance of mediocre advice, their experience of Sedona is shallow. With too many choices and too little time, they find the town nothing more than a checkmark on their "Been there, done that" list.

What a waste. It's a lost chance to touch and be touched by this marvelous place. A waste, because all they really needed was someone they could trust to show them the way. A welcoming friend serving as their local guide and host, giving them the chance to roam freely, laugh lightly, and explore deeply.

Consider this guidebook your friend in Sedona.

Ultimately, I take responsibility for the opinions offered here. In most cases, however, they are based on the views of many. I've interviewed thousands of visitors to gauge their experiences, and I've polled my special team of "Insiders," who helped assemble the latest and best information for this book. These are locals who work within the categories we review. The golf pros, restaurant workers, jeep drivers, retail clerks, and hotel staff that I rely upon around town make *The Insider's Guide to Sedona* truly an inside job. I thank them all.

Sedona is a town that's always changing, so it makes sense to double-check when possible. You'll find ample contact information with which you can do so. If something hasn't been mentioned, I'm happy to hear about it from you. If you agreed with the recommendations, you can also let me know. Visit our website at www.MetaAdventures.com for late-breaking news about everything Sedona. Other contact information is on the inside back flap of this book.

And with that, let me welcome you to my home, one of the planet's most unique places. I hope you'll do it justice by staying as long as you can, and returning again and again. In all my travels around the world, I've found many places that were easy to love. Yet something about Sedona makes it special.

It loves you back.

Happy Trails,
DENNIS ANDRES
SEDONA, ARIZONA

West means West Sedona, not a separate town but a side of town, running along W. Hwy 89A. This side of town is more residential and it also includes the most restaurants.

Uptown is the area on Hwy 89A just north of the intersection with Hwy 179. This is the town's tourist center, full of shops and places to eat and the launching point for jeep tours. In the spring and autumn high seasons, you'll find this area laden with traffic.

OCC indicates the beautiful and historic Oak Creek Canyon, bisected by Hwy 89A, north of the Uptown area. It's especially lovely in the warmer months, when the creek and the shady trees provide respite. Likewise, it is chillier in the colder months, and it receives more snow than the rest of town.

to Flagsta

UPTOWN

89A / Oak Creek Canyon

WEST

the "Y"

89A / West Sedona

to Cottonwood and Jerome

BTY stands for "Below the Y" — the stretch of 179 in Sedona before it intersects with Hwy 89A. Here you find more upscale shopping than in Uptown, as well as excellent art galleries and fine dining. However, it too can fill with traffic on busy days.

Highway 179

VOC

to I-17

VOC is the Village of Oak Creek, nestled around Hwy 179, the strip of highway north of the interstate that is typically your entryway into Red Rock Country. It's your first stop when you arrive and is closest to landmarks like Bell Rock and the Chapel of the Holy Cross. The downside here is that you may feel as if you are commuting to Sedona proper for meals and activities.

ACCOMMODATIONS

S EDONA has no lack of rooms that you can call home during your stay, and the overall level of accommodations here is good and reliable. In the following list, you'll find a few of the outstanding places in town. All other things being equal, it makes sense to choose by which part of town you'd like to stay in. I've broken the list down into five areas.

Upper-end resorts are the most expensive, followed closely by four-diamond B&Bs. Lower-priced resorts follow, moving down the price ladder, then two- and three-diamond B&Bs at par with nicer hotels and country cabins. Motels are the least expensive.

Note a few items that are common in Sedona. Two- and even three-night minimum stays are often required on weekends at those places with fewer rooms, such as cabins and B&Bs. Also, rates often vary by season. Where they don't, go ahead and ask for a discount if you're not coming in the high-season months of spring or autumn. Finally, don't be alarmed by the wide range of rates listed below. Every place in town has figured out that it doesn't hurt to have a high-end suite or deluxe cottage.

HOTELS & MOTELS

WEST I hesitate to tell you about **The Sky Ranch Lodge** because I'm afraid that you'll stay . . . and leave no room for my visiting relatives. It is the best value in town, considering the tremendous views and quiet gardens. Located at the top of Airport Road. $75-$179. 928-282-6400; 888-708-6400. www.skyranchlodge.com ✚ If the most important sensation to you is that new hotel smell, check in at the young **Hampton Inn,** 1800 W. Hwy 89A. 928-282-4700, 800-426-7866. www.hamptoninn.com ✚ If you prefer the smell of the green you'll be saving, visit the inexpensive **Sugar Loaf Lodge** along the same side of the street. $45-$72. 1870 W. Hwy 89A. 928-282-9451, 877-282-0632. www.sedonasugarloaf.com

VOC Let's say you want to save money, and being the active type you'll be outside all day anyway. Try the **Red Rock Lodge** north of the Uptown strip. A cheap sleep, $45-$135 for rooms, $155 and up for a house that sleeps 6. 901 N. Hwy 89A. 928-82-3591. www.redrocklodge.com

✢ For more charm in the heart of it all, consider the **Rose Tree Inn**. Close to everything. $89-$135. 376 Cedar Street. 928-82-2065, 888-282-2065. www.rosetreeinn.com

UPTOWN

Quail Ridge Resort is excellent for families, a couple of couples, or in any situation where more than 2 people want to stay more than 1 night. The chalets have kitchens and there is easy access to the national forest. On the same block as the fancy Graham and Canyon Villa B&Bs, but far less expensive. Tennis court, pool, and barbecue pit too. $96-$194. 120 Canyon Circle Drive. 928-284-9327. www.quailridgeresort.com ✢ Thank goodness that despite a buyout by a timeshare company, they've changed the name back at our local landmark, **Bell Rock Inn & Suites**. $99-$160. 6246 Hwy 179. 928-82-4161, 800-521-3131. www.ilxresorts.com

BTY

You're an artist with a gallery at Hillside or Tlaquepaque about to show your work and you need a reasonable room. Reliable choices along Hwy 179 are the neighboring **Quality Inn Kings Ransom** and the **Comfort Inn**. $79-$149. 771 SR 179. 928-282-7151, 800-846-6164. www.choicehotels.com

✢ The ultimate budget-saver is **Hostel Sedona**. Any cheaper than this and you'd be camping. $15 per night for a bunk bed with your own bed sheet/sleeping bag in their dormitory, or $20 if they provide linens. 928-282-2772.

OCC

Oak Creek Canyon is better known for cabins and cottages than for hotels. An old Arizona favorite is **Don Hoel's Cabins**. 18 cabins, no two alike; larger "family" cabins available too. $80-$135. 9440 N. Hwy 89A. 928-282-3560, 800-292-4635. www.hoels.com ✢ A friend of mine spent her honeymoon at the deluxe suite in **Canyon Wren Cabins**. The marriage didn't last, but the memories did. 4 cabins only. $135-$150. 6425 N. Hwy 89A. 928-282-6900, 800-437-9736. www.canyonwrencabins.com

Although the recent centennial marked the birth of the town with the naming of its post office in 1902, Sedona only incorporated as a city in 1989. Today it straddles two of the largest counties in the country, Coconino and Yavapai.

RESORTS

....

Now that even Holiday Inn has hot tubs and breakfast, you may be wondering what constitutes a "resort" these days. For this book, the Insider defines a resort as a place that has something extra in terms of facilities, such as a tennis court, on-site massage therapists, or workout rooms. Here's who qualifies as the best in this category.

WEST
If pleasure and scenery are the only objects, the best place to stay in town is **Enchantment Resort.** The setting alone—in magnificent Boynton Canyon—is worth the high price, but multiple pools, tennis and croquet courts, good dining, and a brand new spa ("Mii Amo") don't hurt either. The resort is located 7 miles outside of town, which is a pro or a con depending on your point of view. As long as you are paying this much, I'd recommend renting a car you can take on the dirt. Good trails and the interesting Palatki ruins (complete with petroglyphs) are nearby. Of course, there is no lack of tour operators who will do the driving for you. Take note of two minor downsides to this prop-

erty. First, don't count on getting many calls out on your cell phone. (This could be a plus, yes?) Second, the breadth of the property may put you a long walk from the central lobby and dining. (This could also be a plus.) If this is an issue, request a room closer to the center. Third, don't believe them when they say they have an executive golf course: it's too small to be called tiny. $195-$1,045. 525 Boynton Canyon Road. 928-282-2900, 800-826-4180. www.enchantmentresort.com

UPTOWN
The urbane alternative is **L'Auberge de Sedona.** French country cottage style accommodations are complemented by outstanding food, which you can eat creekside when the weather is right. The creek flows gently here, and you'll pass the time peacefully with the ducks amidst the surrounding greenery. The restaurant is exceptional. Note that the Orchards complex is less expensive and not worthy of the 4-star status awarded the main resort. Sitting higher above the creek, its views of the red rocks are superior, but it backs up to the main strip, which is highly trafficked. Make sure to ask about any ongoing renovations so you're not in a room next to a bulldozer. For the cottages or lodge. $230-$380. 800-272-6777. www.lauberge.com

VOC If you believe that what makes a resort is the golf, then the singular choice for you is **The Hilton**. With its purchase of the impressive Sedona Golf Resort and health club, your options for activities are greatly enhanced. The golf club is the best in town, hands down. The restaurant also gets good reviews, but you may find the resort is not quite as well situated in the Red Rocks as you'd like. More often than not, you'll have to step outside to see the best views. $99-$269. 90 Ridge Trail Drive. 928-284-4040, 877-273-3762. www.hiltonsedona.com

BTY The **Radisson Poco Diablo** and **Los Abrigados** are two mid-range resorts offering nice accommodations and central locations. Poco Diablo has a small executive golf course and wonderful views. Nearby is the Twin Buttes formation, backdrop for the Western *Broken Arrow,* starring Jimmy Stewart. $119-$199. 1752 S. Hwy 179. 928-282-7333, 800-333-3333. www.radisson.com/sedonaaz Los Abrigados is also a timeshare property, and it offers the fullest complement of resort benefits in town. Features include a health club and spa, pools, tennis courts, miniature golf, and a bocce court. Part of the property offers access to the creek, and the property sits next door to the town's most exclu-sive shopping galleria, Tlaque-paque. $225-$375 (two homes on property rent for $775 and $1,500). 928-282-1777, 800-521-3131. www.losabrigados.com

OCC The **Junipine Resort** is set deep in Oak Creek Canyon, and that setting is its best feature. The resort rests along the creek, with towering Ponderosa Pines giving it a cooler, greener feel than resorts in town. The suite-size rooms are a good value, and are best taken advantage of by families with children or by multiple couples staying together. It is also close to two of Sedona's most scenic spots, Slide Rock State Park and the West Fork trail. 928-282-3375, 800-742-7463. www.junipine.com ✚ Perhaps the most unique resort accommodation in Sedona is **Garland's Oak Creek Lodge**—so popular, for so long, that they don't need my recommendation. Here it is anyway. During the only months they are open (April through mid-November), you'll dine in heaven and sleep in paradise. No TVs or telephones to disturb you. A very, very long waiting list, but worth the wait. Also, the only clay tennis court for miles around. Oak Creek Canyon. 8067 N. Hwy 89A. 928-282-3343. www.garlandslodge.com

B&Bs AND INNS

Sedona is a fantastic place to stay at a B&B or country inn. I've seen many who've never tried one before become converts upon trying one of the following places. If you are a couple looking for a getaway, and you can afford it, this is my best accommodation recommendation: choose a Sedona B&B for your stay. Why? First, options. The overwhelming majority of Sedona's best B&Bs are right here. Second, quality: the competition has led to increased levels of service at each. At these B&Bs, you'll usually find not only a multiple course breakfast, but an hors d'ouevres hours as well. Frequently the B&B has a pool out back or whirlpool tubs in the room, with a fireplace in the living room. Third, information. Sedona is one town where good advice from locals can maximize your experience. At a B&B, they'll not only know the best restaurants, but will tell you if the chef is sick, or which table is ideal. Here are a few of my favorites.

 WEST On the west side, consider two B&Bs across the street from each other.

Alma de Sedona is among the newest of Sedona's prestige inns, and you can breakfast by the pool, or watch the sunset there in the evening. 12 rooms, $149-$265. 50 Hozoni Drive. 928-282-2737, 800-923-2282. www.almadesedona.com ✚ **Casa Sedona** is a beautiful adobe building, big as B&Bs go with 16 rooms. Views from the property include one of Thunder Mountain, also known as Capitol Butte. 16 rooms, $185-$270. 55 Hozoni Drive., 928-282-2938, 800-525-3756. www.casasedona.com ✚ If what you most enjoy is making friends with locals, the friendliest locals around are Kris and Ed Varjean at the **Lantern Light Inn**. 3 rooms and a condo available, $130-$195, 3085 W. Hwy 89A. 928-282-3419, 877-275-4973. Rarely have so few made so many feel at home so quickly.

UPTOWN Just north of Uptown is the **Wishing Well**.

Where else can you hot tub under the stars, with the lights of town sparkling below you? Have breakfast wheeled to your room the next morning. 5 rooms, $195-$215. 995 N. Hwy 89A. 928-282-4914, 800-728-9474. www.sedonawishingwell.com ✚ Excellent accommodations and a location close to great hiking make the **Apple Orchard Inn** worth considering. 6 rooms, $135-$230. 656 Jordan Road. 928-282-5328, 800 663-6968. www.appleorchardbb.com

VOC The **Graham Inn** and **Canyon Villa** are located on opposite ends of the same semi-circle. "First class" is the word that comes to mind here. Here's Canyon Villa's sales pitch in one sentence: Forget the charm of the rooms just for a moment, and picture yourself lounging by the pool with nothing to block your view of majestic Bell Rock. **11 rooms. $164-$279.** 125 Canyon Circle Drive. 928-284-1226, 800-453-1166. www.canyonvilla.com ✚

Graham Inn & Adobe Village may be the most lauded property in town, and guests leave consistently happy. I am less confident about the value of their private casitas, but not about their luxury. 11 rooms and 4 casitas, **$199-469.** 150 Canyon Circle Drive. 928-284-1425, 800-228-1425. www.sedonasfinest.com ✚

Somewhat more moderately priced is **Adobe Hacienda**, which has a nice dose of green grass (from the neighboring Sedona Golf Resort) to complement the red rocks. 5 rooms, **$169-$219.** 10 Rojo Drive. 928-284-2020, 800-454-7191. www.adobe-hacienda.com

BTY The **Inn on Oak Creek**. You're in the heart of the action here, with the creek behind you and galleries, restaurants, and shops in front. The rooms are exceptionally charming, and the staff is the most consistently friendly, reliable, and dependable in Red Rock Country. Enjoy excellent food by head chef and author Karen Rambo and up-and-comer Martha Upson. While there has been substantial turnover among inn owners in Sedona, the Morris family is here for the long term. Traffic outside on Hwy 179 is a drawback, but the Morrises have done a great job of keeping the sound out and the charm in. 11 rooms, **$180-$275.** 556 Hwy 179. 928-282-7896, 800-499-7896 .www.innonoakcreek.com

OCC North of the Uptown strip is the **Briar Patch Inn.** With 17 cottages on 9 acres, this isn't a traditional B&B, but it does serve breakfast. Rustic, but tastefully decorated. An excellent place if you are looking to leave TV and, yes, even telephones behind. Options for multiple couples or families. **$169-$350.** 3190 N. Hwy 89A. 928-282-2342, 888-809-3030. www.briarpatchinn.com

AIR TOURS

I F YOU THINK SEDONA looks great from the land, you ought to see it from above. My personal preference is to fly in a helicopter, which has greater maneuverability than an airplane. On the other hand, planes are less expensive. My second piece of advice is to stay in the air as long as you can afford—the shortest tours make you feel a bit cheated. If you have the money, try to be up a minimum of 15 minutes in a helicopter, 20 minutes in a plane. Meanwhile, if you want some peace and solitude to really contemplate the views, absolutely nothing beats an hour in a hot air balloon.

The Sedona Airport is easily reached by turning south onto Airport Road off W. Hwy 89A, 1.1 miles west of the "Y." Follow the road up to the top of beautiful Airport Mesa.

PLANES

One company operating at the Sedona Airport offers two types of planes. ✚ Red Rock Biplane Tours is a little more exciting and noisier. Tours are 10 to 45 minutes. $45-$149 per person. ✚ Sky Safari Charter & Air Tours offers the cheapest way to get you in the air at $19 per person for 10 minutes. Other tours take you north to the Grand Canyon ($149 per person) with an add-on of magnificent Lake Powell and Monument Valley. ($209 per person, 4 hours.) Sedona Airport. 928-204-5939, 888-TOO-RIDE. www.sedonaairtours.com

HELICOPTERS

Insiders know to check on how many other people are flying, and which seats you'll be in, to ensure unobscured views. Remember to expect an additional 2.5% airport tax. *(See the "Grand Canyon" essay for details of flights to the natural wonder.)* If you've got more time, money, and a partner, each of these firms offers helicopter picnics for some romance. ✚ Arizona Helicopter Adventures. $48-$128 for 12 minutes up to a half hour. Grand Canyon tour of 2.5 hours for $595. Sedona Airport. 928-282-0904, 800-282-5141. www.arizonahelicopteradventures.com.

HOT AIR BALLOONS

Of the three companies in the area, I recommend the two that are permitted to fly over the Coconino National Forest, which means a lot closer to the red rocks. Their pilots are well qualified, the ride is smooth and quiet, and the views are unforgettable. These morning flights may leave before dawn, which can mean chilly conditions in winter, and will be cancelled if any unusual wind kicks up. Typically, you'll be in the air for an hour, longer if it takes more time to find a good spot to land. Each of the two companies offers a little champagne picnic upon completion of the trip.

If you're lucky, you may observe the distant, 12,000-foot-high, snow-capped San Francisco Peaks during your flight. The baskets can hold a small group of people, but since few folks reserve in advance, the spots seem to all go at once. Please call immediately if you're interested. Meanwhile, be aware of weight and medical restrictions.

Northern Light Balloon Expeditions is the oldest of the area companies. $145 per person. 928-282-2274, 800-230-6222. www.northernlightballoon.com

✚ **Red Rock Balloons** offers a free video per reservation, to help you remember your views from above. $155 per person. 928-284-0040, 800-258-3754. www.redrockballoons.com

SKYDIVING

As "The Insider" of this guide, I've done many things to ensure the quality of this book. I've strapped myself into a Hummer, eaten food I couldn't stand, and hiked hill and valley to find you the most up-to-date information. I draw the line at jumping out of a plane. Add to this that I couldn't find anyone else who has done it either, and so cannot adequately appraise **SkyDive Cottonwood.** They'll allow you to see the Red Rocks (granted, at a distance) while rushing toward the earth for nearly a mile. They specialize in tandem jumping. Since you'll be strapped to an instructor for the jump, you don't need lengthy pre-jump training. Open 7 days a week, by appointment only. Tandem skydive $150, solo jumps available for those with experience. Group rates are available. Video available by appointment. 18 years or older. Cottonwood Airport, 1001 W. Mingus Avenue. 928-649-8899, cell 928-300-2132. www.geocities.com/skydive-cottonwood

ALTERNATIVE HEALTH

I T SEEMS THAT THE LINE between traditional and alternative healing keeps shifting. Chiropractors, once "far out," are now completely mainstream, and no self-respecting city in America is without a host of acupuncturists. In this section we focus on one of Sedona's greatest resources to you as a visitor: a host of individuals and institutions able to facilitate your healing. The good news is that there are many, many helpful folks beyond the ones we've mentioned. The bad news is that people come and go through this town like seedlings in the wind. Combine Insider recommendations with your own good judgment and you'll be able to connect with those that are right for you.

CENTERS

Therapy on the Rocks utilizes the myofascial massage techniques of John Barnes and his staff. Barnes lectures across the country and has a considerable reputation in the field. His approach can be aggressive, even painful at times, but it is done with care and it is effective. Mon-Sat. Opens at 9am, closing times vary. 676 N. Hwy 89A. 928-282-3002. www.myofascialrelease.com

Red Rock Healing Arts Center considers itself a bit more "scientific" in its approach. I've seen especially good results from their massage and healing work. Open daily, 9am-7pm. 251 Hwy 179 in the Creekside Plaza. 928-203-9333, 888-316-9033. www.redrockhealing.com

Arizona Healing Center is probably the longest-lived of Sedona's centers. Their list of offerings includes acupressure, massage, yoga, shiatsu, tai chi, hypnotherapy, NLP, rebirthing, sound therapy, and more. I'd be skeptical: don't count on all of these being available unless you book ahead. It doesn't help that you are just as likely to have a guest pick up the phone as one of the owners when you call. Please check on their extremely Spartan accommodations before signing on to stay overnight. For a low price, you can reserve their sauna for yourself and your friends. 25 Wilson Canyon Road, (In the Uptown area, but very tricky to find. Call for precise directions.) 282-7710, 877-723-2811. www.sedonahealingcenter.com

Sedona Creative Life Center fits the "alternative healing" category if it includes personal growth. The center offers excellent speakers and workshops, quite a few of which focus on healing work. To find out who will be in town when you are, stop by, call them, or visit their website. Mon-Fri 8:30am-5:30pm; other hours for events. 300 Schnebly Hill Road. 928-282-9300. www.sedonacreativelife.com

Two Angels Intuitive Healing offers treatments, consultations and accommodations, including a guest house. These two women combine the intuitive and the scientific, with nutritional counseling among their various skills. P.O. Box 669, Sedona, AZ 86339. 928-204-2083. www.twoangelshealing.com

Metamorphosis Healing Center features Wendy Halliday and other healers on the west side of Sedona. Services include integrative and hot rocks massages and cranial-sacral therapy. Consider a true treat with "A Day at the Spa," which includes a massage, the chi machine, paraffin wax, mud mask and time in the hot tub and flotation tanks, all for $175. Tu-Sun, 10am-6pm, 3195 W. Hwy 89A. 928-282-4834. www.metaspa.com

Dahn Tao Center offers programs including holistic healing, meditation and de-toxification 166 Coffee Pot Drive, 928-282-3600. Mon-Fri, 9am-9pm, Sat 11am-4pm, closed Sunday. www.sedonaretreat.org

Wisdom of the Earth offers pure essential oils for physical, emotional, and spiritual well-being. They offer consultations, seminars, and even study abroad programs in medicinal aromatherapy. One of my few out-of-Sedona recommendations in this book, because what Barry Kapp and Audre Wenzler can teach you about oils and essences is worth the drive. 2680 N. Page Springs Road, Cornville, AZ. 928-649-9968, 888-817-8955. www.wisdomoftheearth.com

Desert Canyon Treatment Center specializes in addiction recovery, although there's word they'll be reaching in other directions too. They offer month-long programs that include outstanding facilitators from around Sedona. This a progressive treatment center that does not use the 12-step method. 8am-5:30pm. 105 Navajo Drive. 928-204-1122. www.desert-canyon.com

The Center for the New Age must be regarded as "iffy" in the healing category, as both the truly gifted and the mainly mediocre have set up shop here in the past. Open 9am-8pm daily. 341 Hwy 179. 928-282-2085. www.sedonanewagecenter.com

RECOMMENDED HEALERS

Jenna Blasi is an outstanding healer practicing Core Synchronism, a version of Cranial-Sacral Therapy. 928-204-2187. ✚ A friend of mine flies all the way from the Midwest for sessions with **Kenyon Crandall**, a Cranial-Sacral specialist. An exceptional healer, she is experienced and very knowledgeable. 928-203-4434. ✚ **Zeffi Kefala** is a gifted medical intuitive. Her energy work is powerful, and she specializes in women's health issues. 928-204-0516. www.ancienthealing.org ✚ **John Chionis** offers Sound Therapy in a gentle yet fascinating treatment. He combines tuning forks and energy work for excellent results. 928-204-1500. ✚ **Divyo** is a wonderful healer who specializes in combining body work and emotional release. Consider the "Harmony" session to undo that physical pain, and the emotional healing comes with it. She's very safe and comforting, and a good listener. 928-204-2489.

SWEAT LODGES

West of Sedona is **Dream Catcher Farm**, where Marcia Kowal facilitates "sweats" for small to large groups. The sweat lodge is a Native American practice used to purify. It involves several sessions inside a hut, sweating out what ails you in intense heat. Definitely not a "try this at home" idea, you'll want to experience this with someone well trained. Marcia discusses the history and meaning of the sweat lodge for those who simply want to try it and directs the process for those who want to use the ceremony for personal shifts. Payment is by donation, but at least $25 per person is appropriate (more if food and lodging are accepted). Vision Quests are available for individuals and groups as well, directed by Marcia and Jorge Arenivar. Jorge is a Yaqui Indian who has studied the Lakota traditions. The approaches of other traditions are welcome. Camping available. 2822 Tissaw Road, Cornville, AZ 86325. 928-646-0257. marciainaz@wildapache.net

HEALTH FOOD

New Frontiers Natural Foods, Sedona's largest health food store, has a good supplements section plus a deli/cafe and juice bar. Open daily, 8am-8pm. Old Marketplace Plaza, 1420 W Hwy 89A. 928-282-6311. www.sedonaoldmarketplace.com

Rinzai's Market is small but is packed with healthy stuff. Owner Rinzai is very knowledgeable. Healthy goodies for lunch, packaged to go. 10am-7pm, Mon-Sat. e-mail rinzais@northlink.com

Basha's, an Arizona grocery chain. 6am-11pm. 160 Coffee Pot Drive in Basha's Plaza. 928-282-5351. www.bashas.com

INSIDE INSIGHT

Creating Your Own Personal Retreat in Sedona

What is so special about Sedona that it allows people to make positive shifts in their life in a seemingly short period of time? Why are even short visits so memorable? Maybe it's the weather, with sunny days year round. Perhaps it is the spectacular scenery that lifts one's spirits. Maybe it's the clean air, which seems to breath new life into people. Don't forget the gentle places to walk, and the lovely, flowing creek. Perhaps there really is a unique energy here that turns your intentions into reality. The statistics show that most of Sedona's tourists (now numbering in the millions) pass through the town, rather than get to know it. Increasingly, however, more of those millions are choosing to stay longer. If you are seeking a place to make changes in your life, Sedona is it. Here I have seen people process the grief of losing loved ones, give up the struggle of bad relationships, release old patterns, and launch new dreams.

"Workshops & Retreats" suggests a few places to consider, but if you're looking for something to do by yourself, here are a few pointers.

1. Set your intention. Before you begin—even if it is on that two-hour drive from the airport—decide what you'd like to focus on during your personal retreat. Is it a health concern that needs attention? Maybe it's a relationship to be ended, or to be created. Is it your career that demands re-thinking? Being clear with your intention will set in motion the people, places, and situations that help create what you desire.

2. Find accommodations first. With a base to start at, you can unpack and relax. This will provide your anchor while you go out and explore. The number one thing that people fail to do to ensure their happiness with lodging is simply to check the room before they commit. If you're making reservations before you come here, get on the web to preview the room. If you're already here, simply ask to see the room. You'll want someplace quiet, preferably with a small fridge. If you can afford it, nothing beats a nice view to wake up to.

3. Buy a journal and write each day. What should you write about? Whatever comes to mind. In fact, write exactly what comes to your mind, and see where it goes. At some point during the day, make sure to write down what you want to end or give up in your life. On a different occasion, list some of the new dreams coming to you.

4. Spend some time in nature. Nture is healing, perhaps because, like our own bodies, it is a complex system, made up of smaller organisms living and working in harmony. When your system is out of balance, placing it in the middle of nature's equilibrium seems to encourage gentle, healthy shifts. In particular, take note of the elements. Spend some time in a place with a gentle breeze or strong wind. Allow yourself to soak up some sunshine. Walk the red earth, and sit upon it. Finally, find your way to Oak Creek and listen to its gentle flow.

5. Listen to some music. A nearby university has launched America's first degree program in healing music. It really does work. So bring a Walkman (for your walks) and a tape player (for the room). You'll find soothing music available throughout town, as well as a number of local musicians whose songs are gentle.

6. Let someone else take care of you. Sedona may be one of the country's foremost sites of alternative healers, massage therapists, and counselors. From individuals to healing centers to treatment institutions, the town is packed with the resources you'll need to create change in your life, all at prices cheaper than in the big city you've come from. Take advantage of them. Likewise look for the town's health food stores. Just as eating poorly can suppress emotions, eating healthfully can be an enormous help in releasing them.

7. Visit Sedona's special places. Among them should certainly be the Chapel of the Holy Cross, the vision of a woman who sought to create a place where people could practice modern spirituality. Go to the places you feel drawn to. This may mean visiting a place with a name that has meaning for you or tracking down a place you've seen in a picture. The town is famous for specific vortex locations, but realize that if there is energy here, the evidence is that it is widespread. Going into Red Rock Country, you simply can't go wrong.

Follow these seven steps with commitment and you'll leave Sedona on the path to your dreams.

ART

YOU'RE IN LUCK. For a small town, Sedona is bursting with art, and it comes in all forms. In fact, if you spent only ten minutes in each gallery, you still wouldn't get to all of them in a weekend. Of course you shouldn't try. Unquestionably, Southwestern art is the strength around here, but I've added some Insider recommendations if you want to explore outside this category. Most galleries open between 9:30 and 10:00 in the morning, and close between 5:00 and 6:00 in the evening. On Sundays most open around noon.

THE ART WALK

I've done the tactical thinking for you so that you can see lots of great art in a savvy, systematic way. Begin by parking at Hillside Center, located a half mile south of the "Y" on Hwy 179. If you are driving toward Sedona from the Village of Oak Creek area, pay attention once you pass the Circle K. Look for the right-hand turn into Hillside.

Begin your stroll through Hillside on the south end with the mixed media art of **Arte-Misia**. ✚ Your next stop on the lower level is the visionary art of the **Terbush Gallery**, but the silver jewelry is especially stunning. ✚ The

Scherer Gallery comes next, a reputable gallery that is strongest in glassware, kaleidoscopes, and the photography of Jack Acory.

Continue around the corner to the **Compass Rose Gallery**. Here you'll see the stunning photographs of Edward Curtiss, whose ambition was to capture images of all the Western tribes. Then be amazed by the fine antique maps, including the ones that show what Arizona was supposed to look like. ✚ Heading up the stairs, the first stop is **Agnisiuh**, which means "Creative Fires" in Sanskrit. This outstanding gallery has particular strength in wood sculptures and inlaid wood "paintings." Look for the rare treats tucked away in its corners, such as the Gibson guitars inlaid with mother-of-pearl Hopi Kachinas. ✚ The sculptures of Stanley "Sandy" Proctor are not only inside **Proctor Fine Art,** they're the chief public art on this level. The paintings featured in this gallery—Joe McFadden's "Saints" collection—are genuinely hard to forget. ✚ Next door is **The Golden Gecko,** which has a fine collection featuring several local artists. The clay animal sculptures of Diana Brewer are a highlight. ✚ The newer galleries on this level are also impressive, including the **Falling Rock Gallery,** featuring Simon Bull's acrylics, and the **Jamie Brice Gallery,** which features the "Hollywood Cowboys" of James Warren.

From Hillside, walk down the exit ramp to **Exposures Gallery** next door. The operative word at Arizona's largest gallery is "big." Big sculptures (I enjoy Bill Worrell's giant shamans), big photographs, big paintings. In fact, if you can go to only one place and you want to see a lot of art, this is the place. ✚ Continue walking south to **Hozho,** where you'll find the **James Ratliff Gallery** upstairs. ✚ The **Lanning Gallery** shows the best contemporary paintings in town. ✚ **Turqoise Tortoise** has some of the Southwest's biggest names, including Navajo sculptor Larry Yazzy and painters C.J. Wells and David Johns.

Much more art awaits you at **Tlaquepaque,** but this assumes you can cross the street safely. Be careful: there's no crossing path, and tourists taking in the scenery aren't always watching the road. Among the number of galleries and shops you'll find here, you should consider the venerable **El Prado,** with its funky wind sculptures and rock chairs, and the **Eclectic Image,** which features hand-tinted and painted photography. ✚ **Mountain Trails** often features sculptors at work.

It's worth it to head up the block to **Visions Gallery** at Creekside Plaza, on the right-hand side of Hwy 179. There Russian-born **Klim and Ia** show off photography, painting, and unique glass pieces in an expansive setting.

Nearby in Uptown are two more worthy stops. The **Sedona Arts Center** always has a show going on, and the gift shop's items are tax-free. **Jordan Road Gallery** features sculpture and offers an eclectic mix of objects. The Center is on the north end of the main drag in Uptown; the gallery is one block west of it on its namesake street. Of course, you could also try this route in reverse, beginning in Uptown at the Arts Center and working your way downhill. Easier on the knees, and you end up at Hillside for lunch or dinner.

Galleries featured in the Art Walk:

+ **Arte-Misia**, Hillside. 671 Hwy 179, Ste BST-4. 928-282-3686.

+ **Terbush Gallery of Sedona**, Hillside. 671 Hwy 179, Ste AST-6. 928-203-4930, 877-203-4925.

+ **Compass Rose Gallery**, Hillside. 671 Hwy 179. 928-282-7904.

+ **The Scherer Gallery**, Hillside. Daily, 10am-5:30pm. 671 Hwy 179. 928-203-9000, 800-957-2673. www.scherergallery.com

+ **Exposures Gallery**, near Hillside. Daily, 9:30am-5:30pm. 561 Hwy 179. 928-282-1125, 800-526-7668. www.ExposuresFineArt.com

+ **James Ratliff Gallery**, Hozho Center. Daily, 9:30am-5:30pm. 431 Hwy 179. 928-282-1404. www.jamesratliffgallery.com

+ **Lanning Gallery**, Hozho Center, Mon-Sat, 9:30am-5:30pm, Sun 10am-5pm. 431 Hwy 179, 928-282-6865 www.lanninggallery.com

+ **The Turqoise Tortoise Gallery**, Hozho Center. 431 Hwy 179. 928-282-2262. www.turqtort-sedona.com

+ **Sedona Artists Studio**, Hozho Center. Mon-Sun 10am-6pm. 431 Hwy 179, Ste B-1. 928-203-0195.

+ **El Prado**, Tlaquepaque. Daily, 9:30am-5pm. 211 Hwy 179, Suite E 101. 928-282-7390, 800-498-3300.

+ **The Eclectic Image**, Tlaquepaque, Mon-Thu,10am-5:30pm Fri & Sat 10am-6pm, Sun 10am-5pm. 928-203-4333. 336 Hwy 179, Ste A 109. www.eclecticimage.com

+ **Mountain Trails Galleries**, Tlaquepaque. 928-282-3225, 800-527-6556. www.MountainTrails.com

+ **Kuivato Gallery** (glassware), Tlaquepaque. 928-282-1212. 800-282-4312. www.kuivato.com

+ **Visions Fine Art**, Creekside Plaza. Daily, 11am-6pm. 251 Hwy 179. 928-203-0022. www.visionsfineart.com

+ **The Sedona Arts Center**, Uptown. Daily, 10am-5pm. 928-282-3865. 15 Art Barn Road. www.sedonaartscenter.com

+ **Jordan Road Gallery**, Uptown. Mon-Sat 10am-5pm, Sun 12noon-5pm. 305 Jordan Road. 928-282-5690. www.jordanroadgallery.com

BARGAIN HUNTING

For great deals, head to the west side of town to the **Art Mart**, where you can buy direct from many local artists. Mon-Sat, 10am-6pm; Sun 11am-6pm. 2081 W. Hwy 89A in the Harkins Theater plaza. 203-4576. www.art-mart-sedonaarizona.net

Sedona Trading Post is an interesting alternative in the Village of Oak Creek. Southwestern focus. Paintings, metalwork, jewelry. Daily, 9am-6pm. 10 Bell Rock Plaza, Suite A. www.sedonatradingpost.com

OUTSTANDING LOCAL ARTISTS

Sculptor **Susan Kliewer** (whose work is available in town) created the rendition of Sedona Schnebly that stands at the public library. Renowned artist **John Soderberg** sculpts even bigger pieces. **Tony Carrito** the creator of "Scarfati," is represented at The New West Gallery. **Marliss Powell** is a contemporary artist who designed the panels on the Sedona Arts Center in Uptown, while resident **Joe Beeler** is one of the founders of the Cowboy Artists of America. **Mike Medow** is currently "hot" but tough to find, since he does not seek gallery representation. However, his work can be seen at Enchantment Resort. **Joe Wise** stands out among watercolor painters, while **Paul Blasi** is a young and talented glass-blower. Sedona is home to some splendid works of photography, with the focus obviously on landscapes. Look for **Lou DeSerio**'s pieces, along with those of **Tom Johnson** of *Sedona Magazine,* light-chaser **Michael Irvine**, and **Larry Lindahl**, the man-on-the-rocks for *Arizona Highways.*

(See "Events" for the Sedona Arts Festival and the Sculpture Walk held each autumn.)

PRIVATE TOURS

Tara Golden of Wet Paint Studio offers art tours in Sedona. Tara takes you to the workshops of up to three local artists to help you understand their creative processes. Stops at Sedona galleries are sometimes included. 3 hours, $75 per person. 928-203-4156. www.sedonaarttours.com

TIPS ON BUYING ART

If you're new to buying art, consider two tips from the pros. First, understand that art is generally not a great investment, financially speaking. Buy something because you like it, not because you think it will appreciate in monetary value. Avoiding making purchases for art that is hot or trendy, but not your preference. Second, use your money to buy the "most" art you can. It's better to choose one great piece for $1,000 than five pieces for $200 each. Meanwhile, if your time or mobility are limited, buy a copy of Sedona Magazine and peruse the advertisements. Many high-end galleries advertise inside; read how they describe themselves before you decide which galleries to visit.

b

BIRDWATCHING

Perhaps without realizing it, you've entered a birdwatcher's paradise. First, Sedona has a tremendous variety of terrain within a small area, and that means seeing lots of different birds without having to go far. Second, pleasant weather and beautiful scenery makes it especially easy and enjoyable to watch the birds.

If you'd like a little orientation and guidance, your best bets are definitely the two local Arizona state parks. If you feel ready to go off on your own, then I advise you to pick any of the area's hiking trails. Wherever you go, start out early, take water, dress appropriately, and good luck!

BIRDS TO SEE

Among the many wonderful birds to look for, let me name just a few to whet your appetite while the **Turkey Vultures** (they call them buzzards in Texas) soar overhead. Birds of prey include the **Red-tailed Hawk** and the small falcon known as the **American Kestrel.** The **Eagle** and **Blackhawk** make Sedona their home, but you'll need some luck to see one. You may see a few **Roadrunners** but more often the roads host families of **Gambel's Quail** running across the street. Whether or not you hear the sad call of the **Mourning Dove** in the trees, you'll almost certainly encounter the noisy **Scrub Jay** or its black-crested cousin, the **Stellar's Jay.** In the same zones, look for the beautiful **Western Bluebird** and the **Bullock's Oriole.** Those big black birds soaring above aren't crows: they're **Common Ravens.** During the day, with your eye on Sedona's beautiful wildflowers, you may notice the small **Black-Chinned** or **Green-Throated Hummingbirds.** By contrast, it is the dark of night that the **Great Horned Owl** prefers. Count yourself lucky if you see one. In areas along the creek, look for small **Kingfishers** perched on branches as you await the large and graceful **Great Blue Heron,** which looks like it belongs in the Everglades.

PLACES TO GO

Red Rock State Park offers morning outings twice a week. The park has both riparian and high desert sections, allowing for a nice variety of bird habitats. In addition, the walking paths are quite gentle here. Walks are typically on Wednesday and Saturday, at either 7am or 8am, depending on the season. These walks cater to everyone. Bring binoculars if you have them; a few may be available to borrow. $5 per vehicle entrance fee. Drive west from the "Y" on Hwy 89A for 5 miles to Lower Red Rock Loop Road. Continue a few miles to the park entrance on the right. 928-282-2202. www.pr.state.az.us/parkhtml/-redrock.html

Slide Rock State Park hosts a bird walk on Saturdays when they have enough personnel. Remember that the park is up Oak Creek Canyon, so allow time if you're coming from the west side or the Village of Oak Creek. This Arizona State Park is also by Oak Creek but 1,000 feet higher in elevation, so you'll see a completely different set of birds here. $8 entrance fee per vehicle. Go 7 miles north on Hwy 89A from the "Y." 928-282-3034. www.pr.state.az.-us/parkhtml/slide-rock.html

The list of places to watch birds may be nearly infinite in just this small area, but an Insider favorite is **Page Springs Hatchery**, outside of town. Call 928-634-4805 for directions.

SUPPLIES

Sedona Sports offers birding books and binoculars, including the nifty kind that automatically self-focus. (Ah, technology.) The store also has walking sticks for sale or rent. Across from Tlaquepaque, 251 Hwy 179. 928-282-1317.

Canyon Outfitters is a good choice for binoculars if you are on the west side of town. Hydration packs and plenty of good hiking advice are available. 2701 W. Hwy 89A. 928-282-5293.

EVENTS

The annual **Verde Valley Birding & Nature Festival** is custom-designed for your birdwatching pleasure. Although Dead Horse State Park in Cottonwood is the primary venue, Red Rock State Park and Slide Rock State Park in Sedona also participate. The festival is held on the last weekend in April (25-27 in 2003) and includes field trips, workshops, and bird counts. Over 171 species were seen in 3 days last year. Field trips included the Grand Canyon to see condors; viewing birds from the Verde Canyon Railroad train; and "power birding" in Prescott. Call Barbie Hart, the enthusiastic coordinator of the event, at 928-282-2002. You can reach a special line at the City of Cottonwood, Parks & Recreation, 928-634-8437. www.birdyverde.org

BOOKS & BOOKSTORES

N EED A NEW COPY of *The Insider's Guide* for a friend? Here are the places to look for it, and for other good books too.

GENERAL

The Worm has many local and regional titles and is found at the foot of Uptown. It is Sedona's largest and oldest full-service book and music store. Daily, 9am-9pm. 207 N. Hwy 89A. 928-282-3471.

The Storyteller Bookstore has the charm of a small place crammed with good stuff. Plenty of area titles. Daily, 10am-5pm. Tlaquepaque, 336 Hwy 179, B-105. 928-282-2144.

Sedona Books & Music is broad-based and is run by local author and historian Kate Ruland-Thorne. Mon-Fri 9:30am-5:30pm, Sat & Sun 9:30am-3:30pm. Basha's Shopping Center, corner of Hwy 89A and Coffee Pot Drive. 928-203-0711.

The Book Loft just south of the "Y" is a local institution and also offers used books. 10am-6pm daily, except closed on Tuesdays. 175 Hwy 179. 928-282-5173.

Traders Gallery is an antique dealer, but they also stock used, rare, and metaphysical books. Mon-Fri 10am-5pm. 2550 W. Hwy 89A, #4, 928-282-1736.

METAPHYSICAL

Golden Word offers a good music collection and listening center along with books. A very pleasant setting. Sun-Wed 10am-7pm, Thu-Sat 10am-8pm. 3150 W. Hwy 89A, corner of Dry Creek Road. 928-282-2688.

Crystal Magic has videos for rent plus books. A very good collection. Mon-Sat 9am-9pm, Sun 9am-8pm. 2978 Hwy 89A. 928-282-1622.

Crystal Castle is Sedona's "Metaphysical Department Store" and it has an excellent variety. Across from Tlaquepaque. Mon-Fri 9am-7pm, Sat & Sun 9am-8pm. 313 Hwy 179. 928-282-5910.

Center for the New Age has improved its collection. Across from Tlaquepaque. Daily, 9am-8pm. 341 Hwy 179. 282-2085.

SEDONA-RELATED BOOKS

A few recommendations, admittedly highly biased.

The Call of the Canyon, by Zane Grey. The Western classic that put Oak Creek Canyon on the map tells the story of a man from New York who comes to find himself. Little did Grey know that story would be repeated a few thousand times in the years to come. Currently out of print according to Amazon.com but available in audio format.

Sedona: The Most Remarkable Place on Earth, by Tom Johnson. A beautiful coffee-table photo book by resident pro Tom Johnson. A great gift or a great souvenir.

Sedona Through Time: Geology of the Red Rocks, by Wayne Ranney. If you want to get to the bottom of how the place came to be this color, check out this geological guide.

Sedona: Treasure of the Southwest, by Kathleen Bryant. The town's best historical writer teamed with fantastic photos and a low price make this a perfect gift book.

Tacos y Mas, recipes by Chef Karen Rambo, text by Carol Haralson, and photography by Paula Jansen. Chef Rambo is one of Sedona's finest. This colorful book contains dozens of her ideas for stuffing a tortilla plus some of her signature salsas, marinades, pestos, and sides. In book-stores and at the Inn on Oak Creek B&B, 556 Hwy 179, where Rambo serves breakfast 3 days a week. Go in and get her to sign one.

What Is a Vortex? A Practical Guide to Sedona's Energy Sites, by Dennis Andres. The best-selling book in town discusses Sedona's energy in a practical yet spiritual way. But who's that author? In gift shops and bookstores regionally, or call 928-204-1560.

A Window on Sedona, by Dottie Webster and Pamela Morris, photographed by Paula Jansen and edited by Carol Haralson. See how Sedonans have taken the beauty outside and mixed it with their own taste and culture to make beautiful places to live. In gift shops and bookstores regionally, on Amazon.com, or through Cinnamon Stone Publishing, PO Box 4189, Sedona, AZ 86340.

Recipes from Sedona's Heartline Café, by Chef Charles Cline. Chuck and his wife, Phyllis, launched the Heartline in 1991 in a former biker's hangout, and it has become a favorite of locals and out-of-towners. Interestingly illustrated, with 125 recipes for diners' favorites. Not widely distributed in bookstores, but signed copies always available at the restaurant, 1610 W. Hwy 89A.

BREAKFAST

ONLY ON VACATION do most of us get a chance to dawdle over the morning meal. Find a spot for coffee or for a classic hot American breakfast with eggs and the works. Get cozy. Settle in. Shake out the *Red Rock News* and smile at the nice waitress. From some tables you'll even be able to glance out at a Red Rock vista while buttering your toast.

Let's handle the caffeine addicts first.
If you can't begin your day without a cup of java, then here are the best places to begin.

Ravenheart opens at 6am. Old Market Place Plaza, 1379 W. Hwy 89A. 928-282-5777.

Sedona Coffee Roasters opens at 6am. The new owner has made positive changes. 2155 W. Hwy 89A. 928-282-0282.

I remember thinking many, many years ago, "All it will take for me to move here is a good bagel place." And voila! Now we have a great choice on the west side. If you plan a picnic or outdoor hike, consider grabbing your afternoon sandwich to go from either place.

New York Bagels and Donuts, open at 6am daily, has great, fresh bagels just like back East. 1650 W. Hwy 89A.

Okay, enough with coffee and donuts. Let's say you want a real meal. .

The Coffee Pot is our oldest and most famous breakfast spot. Parking is iffy (you might have to park at the movie theater across the street on a Sunday morning), but you'll have more than 100 omelette choices when you enter. 2050 W. Hwy 89A. 928-282-2626.

The Airport Restaurant at the top of Airport Road has good food and great scenery. It begins serving at 7am for early risers who'd like to watch the sunrise from Airport Mesa. You can watch planes take off from their outdoor seating area. Daily 7am-9pm. Breakfast 7am-11pm, Sun 7am-12noon. 928-282-3576.

Desert Flour Bakery satisfies all your wildest fantasies in baked goods. Splendid pastries. Mmm! Serves cappuccino, too. Village of Oak Creek, 6446 Hwy 179. 928-284-4633.

L'Auberge de Sedona. You'd expect good French toast from the French restaurant in Uptown, and you'll get it, plus fine service and many other good dishes. This is the class act of breakfast in town. 301 L'Auberge Lane. 928-282-1661.

Garland's Oak Creek Lodge. The Insider secret for breakfast is definitely Garland's. Up front, I'll tell you that the chances you'll get in are slim. But if they have room, and you'd like something delicious in a great old lodge, call Garland's. In fact, call well ahead and bring an empty stomach for a unique, multiple-course meal that usually includes waffles, eggs, tortillas, or fresh local trout. Order as much as you like, all for $10-$12. Open spring through autumn. 8 miles from Uptown, 8067 N Hwy 89A. 928-282-3343.

New Frontiers is the place for you if good health is your priority. Grab a grain muffin and a wheat grass shot from the deli counter/juice bar. Daily 8am-8pm. Breakfast 7am-2pm. Old Marketplace, 1420 W. Hwy 89A. 928-282-6311.

SUNDAY BRUNCH

Here are a few of my favorite places for brunch. Come hungry, or don't come at all.

L'Auberge de Sedona offers two seatings, at 11am and 3pm. Nice atmosphere close to Oak Creek. $35 per person; children half price. Uptown, 301 L'Auberge Lane. 928-282-1661.

Enchantment Resort offers a wonderful brunch with great views of Boynton Canyon at the Yavapai Restaurant. 10:30am until 2:15pm. $29.50 per person; half-price for children 6-12 years of age. Beyond the west side of town, 525 Boynton Canyon Road. 928-282-2900.

Raddison Poco Diablo Resort allows you to look out over its green grass golf course as you eat. 11am-2pm. $25 per person; $12.50 for children under 12. 1752 Hwy. 179. 282-7333, 800-333-3333.

CAMPING

WELCOME to the Great Outdoors! The smell of ponderosa pine, the touch of cool creek water, and the howl of the coyote will tickle your senses in Sedona. The major change in recent years has been the prohibition on freestyle camping through a large portion of the local forests. In exchange, the Forest Service has constructed a few new official campsites to accompany the old-time spots in Oak Creek Canyon. It eliminates a bit of our freedom, but it should prevent some of the damage to the forests that had been taking place. For more nature and less civilization, I like Pine Flats, which is far up into the canyon. Here a spring of tasty clean water flows just to the side of the road, and you can nestle on pine needles under the tall ponderosas. Campground cost is $15 per night. Although all developed campgrounds are excluded from the Red Rock Pass, a separate site fee is required *(see "Parks and Passes" for details)*. Call the Ranger Station at 928-282-4119 or stop by their office on Brewer Road (close to the "Y") for details. For reservations (recommended), call the National Recreation Reservation Services at 877-444-6777.

C A M P S I T E S

	campsites	water	toilets	season	reservations	trailers
Bootlegger	10	no	no	Apr 15-Oct 31	not taken	no
Cave Springs *has showers*	82	yes	yes	Apr 15-Oct 31	taken	yes, to 36 ft.
Chavez Crossing	3 group	yes	yes	all year	taken	yes, to 40 ft.
Manzanita	18	yes	no	all year	not taken	no
Pine Flats	57	yes	yes	Mar 1-Nov 15	taken	yes, to 36 ft.

Note that "Banjo Bill" along Oak Creek is no longer an overnight campground. For further information, write Coconino National Forest, Sedona Ranger District, P.O. Box 300, Sedona, AZ 86339-0300. www.redrockcountry.org

THE WILDER SIDE

If you were hoping to escape even these signs of civilization, then you can head in one of three directions for camping. South, you can camp in the Beaver Creek area of I-17. North, go beyond the Oak Creek Vista and camp off Hwy 89A. East, you can camp between I-17 and Schnebly Hill Vista.

SUPPLIES

Canyon Outfitters has a nice collection of tents and backpacks upstairs, as well as cookware, water filters, shoes, clothing, headlamps, and books on the first floor. 2701 W. Hwy 89A. 928-282-5293.

Sedona Sports lacks the tents, but does have other helpful gear, including backpacks, water purification equipment, and mess kits. They also specialize in CamelBak hydration packs and have a very good selection of hiking boots. Across from Tlaquepaque, 251 Hwy 179. 928-282-1317.

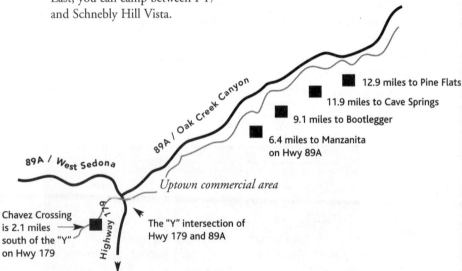

12.9 miles to Pine Flats

11.9 miles to Cave Springs

9.1 miles to Bootlegger

6.4 miles to Manzanita on Hwy 89A

89A / Oak Creek Canyon

89A / West Sedona

Uptown commercial area

Chavez Crossing is 2.1 miles → south of the "Y" on Hwy 179

Highway 179

The "Y" intersection of Hwy 179 and 89A

The exit onto I-17 is 15 miles from the "Y" on Hwy 179

CAR RENTALS

I F YOU DIDN'T RENT A CAR at the airport in Phoenix, or if you'd just like something fun to drive in, Sedona has a few options for you. Given the limited public transportation here (read: non-existent, I'd recommend any of these places to get some wheels.

CAR RENTALS

Enterprise Rent-A-Car is the only nationally branded agency in town. Reliable and inexpensive, they also offer to pick you up. Close to Circle K, 2550 W. Hwy 89A. 928-282-2052. National Reservations, 800-736-8222. www.enterprise.com

Practical Rent-a-Car is a cheap option, with a selection ranging from their inexpensive Chevy Metro ($19 per day including mileage) to large minivans and a couple 4WD autos. They also offer pick-up and drop-off. 60 Tortilla Dr. in West Sedona (turn right off 89A at the Giant station. 928-282-0554. rentalcar@hotmail.com

Sedona Jeep & Car Rentals is good, especially if you are lucky enough to be flying directly into Sedona Airport, where they are located. Daily 8-5pm. Sedona Airport, 235 Terminal Drive. 928-282-2227. www.sedonajeeprentals.com

JEEP RENTALS

If you'd like to grab the wheel your-self, Sedona has no lack of interest-ing roads rough enough for you. Cruise out to the Honanki Indian Ruins or up Sedona's historic Schnebly Hill Road for some awe-some views. The following compa-nies provide maps and details.

Sedona Jeep & Car Rentals: $60 for 3 hours, $100 for 8:30am-3:30pm, $130 for 24 hours. Sedona Airport, 235 Air Terminal Drive. 928-282-2227, 800-879-5337. www.sedonajeeprentals.com

LaVista Jeep Rental is at the La Vista Motel at the north end of Uptown. $59.99 for 2 hours, $79.99 for 4 hours, $99.99 for 8 hours, $129.99 for 24 hours. 500 N. Hwy 89A. 928-282-0000.

Canyon Jeep Rentals: $69.95 for 5 hours, $89.95 for 10 hours, $99.95 for 24 hours. Oak Creek Terrace, across from Dairy Queen. Oak Creek Canyon, 4548 N. Hwy 89A. 928-282-6061.

COFFEE & CYBERCAFES

COFFEE

Ravenheart is the new king of coffee, with a splendid interior and comfy atmosphere. Truffles and other chocolate goodies are hard to resist. Angela is the sweetheart manager who will make you feel welcome. Open 6am-11 pm daily, even holidays. Old Marketplace Plaza, 1370 W. Hwy 89A. 928-282-5777.

Sedona Coffee Roasters is the old stand-by of locals, and it has a nice view from the deck. On 89A, next to the Harkins Theatre complex. Each morning they have a number of very good blends, including flavored. Mon-Sat 6am-5pm, Sun 6am-3pm. 2155 W. Hwy. 89A. 928-282-0282.

The Brew at the View is next door to Pink Jeeps. Have a sip here while you wait for your tour. Better, after your jeep tour since there are no bathrooms on the way. Daily, 7am-4pm. Uptown, 204 N. Hwy 89A. 928-282-4354.

Plaza Café could just as easily be in Berlin, Geneva, or Florence, given the Euro ex-pats who hang out there. Espresso, cappuccino, and the like, plus exceptionally healthy café meals made fresh each day. 1449 W. Hwy 89A. 928-203-9041.

Creative Juices is a good choice in the Village of Oak Creek. They offer the indulgence of Krispy Kreme doughnuts alongside the healthfulness of fresh juices. Good coffee with a nice decor. Mon-Thu 6:30am-4pm, Fri-Sun 6:30am-5pm. Tequa Plaza, 7000 Hwy 179. 928-284-5290.

CYBERCAFES

Having traveled in more than 40 countries, I find it depressing to report that the worst public access to the web may be right here in the USA. Here are several local options.

CyberSedona has 5 computers. 15 cents a minute, with a 15-minute minimum. Mon-Thu 10am-9pm, Fri-Sat 10am-10pm, Sun 12pm-8pm. Basha's Shopping Center, 162A Coffee Pot Drive. 928-282-7368. www.cybersedona.net

Ravenheart has only a pair of computers, but the most comfy chairs and atmosphere.

Sedona Coffee Roasters has high speed access on its 2 computers. $2.50 per 15 minutes.

Sedona Public Library has several computers available, but the free access seems to guarantee that they are always occupied. Mon 12pm-8pm, Tu & Thu 10am-6pm, Wed 10am-8pm, Fri-Sat 10am-5pm. 3250 White Bear Road. 928-282-7714.

DAY SPAS & MASSAGE

A S LONG AS YOU'RE HERE TO RELAX, you might as well go all out. Sedona is blessed with an extremely large number of people who are well trained in taking care of you. Whether you're gearing up for a wedding or gearing down after a day on the trails, the following people and places will help you look and feel great.

DAY SPAS

Sedona has plenty of places to pamper you. Among the choices offered re those connected with the resorts, which are more than adequate. However, for the very best spots, I interviewed dozens of locals and visitors who found the following out-of-the-way spots best.

Colour Line Studio is praised by local ladies. Mary Ann does a nice job cutting hair and Kelly is recommended for massage. Said one happy client, "It's half the price and twice the quality. Everything they do is top of the line. Everything." They offer authentic European facials and organic products. It's a full-service salon, although there is no Jacuzzi or mud-bath. Very receptive to wedding groups. **2860 Hopi Drive. 928-203-1780. www.colourlinestudio.com**

Red Rock Healing Arts offers facials and body polishes—your basic day-spa treatments supplemented by more interesting approaches. For example, live blood analysis is available, to see what's going on inside you. ($50, 30 min-1 hour, plus a consultation showing your blood cells on a TV screen.) If there's something inside you don't like, the "Oxygen cabinet" can steam it out of you ($40 for 1 hour; $10 discount if combined with other treatments). Ushi (that's a person, not a treatment), combines acupressure with other techniques, is recommended among a group of good massage therapists. **251 Hwy 179. 928-203-9933. www.redrockhealing.com**

Lovejoy's Enchanted Cottage is the office of expert holistic manicurist and pedicurist Deb Lovejoy. She works on your soles...and your soul. **485 Coffee Pot Drive. 928-282-7667, 928-300-9003.**

New Day Spa is Sedona's newest entry in the category, and it is full of good healing energy. Cozy inside, the body work is on par with Mii Amo, the high priced spa at Enchantment Resort. Osho Plaza, 1449 W. Hwy 89A. 928-282-7502.

HAIR SALONS

A top choice of Sedona women is **Raymond Rodriguez Salon.** Raymond charges $45 for a cut. **Shinar** is also good; she charges $38. 2155 Shelby Drive, 928-204-5545. **Mark Owen Salon** gets very good reviews. 431 Hwy 179. 928-282-1564.

Although interest in Sedona's mystical energy dates back decades, the New Age community made its mark here in the 1980s. At the start of that decade psychic/channel Page Bryant coined the term "vortex," giving a name to the phenomenon that so many had reported. Many consider author and workshop leader Dick Sutphen to be the father of Sedona's New Age community. He published several books on this and other esoteric topics.

RECOMMENDED MASSAGE THERAPISTS

Although people often look to institutions for safe choices, the irony in Sedona is that some of the least experienced healers will be found there. When people get established and experienced, they often leave. Considering how little they get paid at these centers, who can blame them?

Jean Neesley does a variety of sessions, but considers the "Hot Rocks" massage her specialty. The only one among our recommended therapists with a private office (most others come to you or treat you in a room of their own home), located in 2756 Plaza del Oro, W. Hwy 89A. 928-204-1099. It's always a good sign if the locals like somebody. That's why **Lin Huntting** is a smart bet, and she's available for visitors, too. 928-204-0845. **Patricia Flores** uses her "Mayan Healing Hands" for an excellent, healing massage. 928-282-2524. I recommend **Vance Blow**, especially for a good sports massage. 928-282-4626. Work with any of them and you'll come back with a smile!

DINING OUT

THERE'S SOMETHING ABOUT SEDONA that draws couples who want to make their culinary dreams come true. Great restaurants have been opened here by a pair from San Francisco and two more from Los Angeles, a couple from New Jersey and another from Chicago, and two women from the Pacific Northwest. All have turned their aspirations into fine restaurants. The result is a nice number of dining choices for a town of this size. Besides my specific recommendations below, the key advice I would add is to call ahead. Throughout the spring and autumn, and on weekend nights the rest of the year, the influx of visitors makes it tough to get a table at Sedona's best spots. Expected attire in Sedona covers the wide range from casual to "resort casual." So wear shoes and look clean if you can; but they won't boot you out if you've just come in off a trail.

EXCEPTIONAL FINE DINING

I'd put each of these in my highest category, for consistently good food and service. All would be considered "fine dining" in terms of price. Reservations essential.

René at Tlaquepaque On those rare occasions when I have a date, I'll take her to René at Tlaquepaque, the choice for a leisurely, romantic dinner in Sedona. The dining room re-decoration in 2002 didn't hurt the pleasant atmosphere, which features landscape paintings of Sedona and the West. There's a nice sense of space between the tables and within the booths. The cuisine is called Continental, but more specifically I would call it "France comes to the Southwest and settles in at Sedona." Consider that along with rack of lamb (house specialty) or venison in a whisky juniper berry sauce you can have a Seitan Tofu Wellington. Other choices include grilled ahi tuna, cedar plank salmon, Dover sole, and Idaho trout in seafood; filet mignon, as well as beef, venison, veal, and pork tenderloins; free-range chicken picatta and roast duck; and a delicious sweet potato ravioli. If you think I'm giving the menu away before you get there, don't worry: how each is prepared and what it is served with is a story you'll want to read. Entrée prices are $19-$26, except for the rack of lamb for two, which is carved tableside and costs $65. Owner Deborah Leatherwood is the kind hostess and partner Chef Walter Paulson handles the cooking. You won't be rushed here: even if you aren't dressed formally, they'll serve you as if this meal were really important. The wine list is extensive but also expensive: they are perhaps taking advantange of the popularity of some distinct varieties that, although special, need not be priced so high. The outdoor seating in the courtyard is nice, especially for lunch. Afterwards, take a stroll though Tlaquepaque. **Accepts V, MC. Tlaquepaque Village, 336 Hwy 179. 928-282-9225. www.rene-sedona.com**

Dahl & DiLuca Ristorante Italiano Now let's say my date is bringing her visiting parents, and I want to show all of them a good time and demonstrate my exceptional good taste. I take them to Dahl & DiLuca, which provides a tremendous atmosphere in which to have a fantastic Tuscan meal. After all, I've got another date, and that's worth celebrating! The D&D formula is "not to over-complicate the dish." It works. The pasta is made fresh daily and tastes it. Veal (vitello) is a house specialty, prepared piccata, parmigiana, marsala, and Botticelli and ranges in price from $22-$26. Try the prawns spiedini if you object to veal. Note that hard floors make theis restaurant slightly livelier and louder than others. On a singular occasion I know of, a couple thought it too loud. In every other case people find it lively and entertaining, and they recognize that a full restaurant means good food is being served. It's a nice touch when Lisa Dahl sings by the piano while her husband, Italian-born chef Andrea DiLuca, cooks in the kitchen. **Open 5pm daily. Accepts V, MC, AE, D. 2321 W Hwy 89A. 928-282-5219. www.dahl-diluca.com**

Shugrue's Hillside Grill When I just don't know what people want, I send them to Shugrue's Hillside Grill. The only way to go wrong here is not to go. I like Shugrue's incredible consistency, found in both the menu items and the professional servers. Often voted Sedona's best seafood, although other offerings are also excellent, such as the steaks and rack of lamb. The seafood selection is prodigious. Soft shell crabs, salmon, Pacific mahi mahi, "colossal" scallops, halibut and ahi can be grilled, sautéed or blackened and are accompanied by soup, salad or chowder, among other items. Lobster or shrimp scampi (flame-broiled, a signature dish) can be had with a petite fillet.

Kiwi shrimp is a twist, and risotto del mar rounds out the offerings. My only disappointment is the *paella,* but then again, I can't find anyone else in America who makes it as well as the nice Spanish lady I know. Pepper steaks and filets, rack of lamb, chicken, portabello mushrooms, vegetables (mesquite grilled), and ravioli complete a weighty menu. Entrees $20-$30. I recommend the panoramic views from their deck if the weather is right. If it's too chilly, then sit inside by the glass wall. Usually there's some entertainment on weekends. My mother, who can't cook well but sure knows how to order, loves the salads and the Turkey Reuben for lunch. **Reservations essential, especially for those views. Accepts V, MC, AE, D. Hillside Plaza, 671 Hwy 179. 928-282-5300. www.hillsidesedona.com, click on Shugrue's.**

Piñon Bistro There's very little I've recommended outside of Sedona, in this chapter or in any other. Pinon Bistro is the exception that's worth the drive. Excellent, fresh, reliable. While they offer only 4-5 entrees per night, the menu is sufficiently varied to serve any taste, and dishes are prepared to perfection. Menu changes weekly. If it looks different than the last time you were here, that's because they're hanging someone else's paintings now. **Drive west on Hwy 89A to Cottonwood and turn left at the intersection of Hwy 260, then drive a half-block up and look for it on the left-hand side of the street. Serves dinner only; no entertainment. Open Thu-Sun; closed much of the summer. Cash/checks only. 1075 Hwy 260, Cottonwood. 928-649-0234.**

Garland's Oak Creek Lodge You'll be an insider yourself if you can get into Garland's, deep in Oak Creek Canyon. The lodge is usually full, with guests returning year after year for the pleasant surroundings and exquisite meals prepared by Amanda Stine, self-taught chef for two decades at Garland's. Featuring up to 6 courses, dinner is a set menu in an atmosphere that is "relaxed and elegant." The menu is set, but they'll probably let you know what it will be when you call. Courses include a unique homemade bread, rich soup, and delicate salad to begin with. Ingredients include vegetables from their own gardens (they made a string bean lover out of me), and they use their own peaches in the daiquiris. Visit their garden and greenhouse to see for yourself. Entrees have included rack of lamb, grilled fillet of beef (with a gorgonzola butter that is incredible), baby back ribs, grilled salmon, grilled halibut, and chicken scallopini. Dessert always changes, but the taste is always delicious. It's important to note that if you do get into Garland's you probably won't have the table to yourself. Cocktails begin at 6pm, and at 7pm you'll find your way to your assigned table with two other people, most likely guests staying at the lodge. Most people like it that way, but Garland's will try to seat you alone if you request it. Call ahead. Better yet, call far ahead. **$29-$35, not including drinks. Open April through mid-November. Accepts V, MC. Look for the sign on the left as you drive north 8 miles from Uptown, 8067 N. Hwy 89A. 928-282-0785. www.garlandslodge.com**

MORE FINE DINING: GREAT FOOD & ATMOSPHERE

Heartline Café is the place I like to take visiting friends who come to Sedona to refresh body and soul. Heartline perfectly balances the relaxation you want to feel on vacation with the high standards with which you hope to be fed. The almond-crusted trout is the delicious specialty of the house: I absolutely ate the whole thing. Meanwhile, the salads are a delicious value, including the watercress with grapes and pistachios in a sherry vinaigrette; the spinach with gorgonzola, pecans, and sun-dried tomato vinaigrette; and even the horrible-sounding-but-delicious-eatin' warm cabbage. Some come thinking this place specializes in health food—perhaps an inference from the restaurant's name—but this is an illusion that

can only be maintained until the fabulous desserts arrive. The chief gripe here is the small parking lot. If it's full at dinner time, I say don't even bother pulling in: park next door at Ace Hardware. Like the food? Buy the cookbook, sold at the bar. **Entrees $14-$28. Open daily for dinner at 5pm. Lunch served 11am-3pm, but not served on Tu, Wed. Accepts V, MC, AE, D. 1610 W. Hwy 89A. 928-282-0785. www.heartlinecafe.com**

Robert's Creekside Cafe & Grill
When Regis Philbin's wife tasted the peach cobbler here, she liked it so much she went on national television to tell the world about it. You couldn't get a table if you were the Pope that week, but the surge has slowed while the food remains very good. Beware of wonderful salads that leave no room for your entrée. There is some outdoor seating, but with the balcony overhanging the creek, the views are best by day. There's a guitar player or other light music for entertainment on many nights. **251 Hwy 179. 928-282-3671.**

L'Auberge de Sedona is the only place in town where gentlemen need to wear a jacket (and only on Saturday night). The resort's restaurant is close to the creek, and lunch can be had on the terrace next to it. The French-cuisine menu is very rich and changes weekly. A la carte or elegant prix fixe dining are available.

lunch

Outstanding service. Breakfast, lunch and dinner daily, with brunch on Sunday. Accepts AE, D, V, MC. 301 L'Auberge Lane, 282-1667. www.lauberge.com

Savannah is named for the owners' young daughter. This establishment opened in 2002 and wasted no time: it immediately became Sedona's best steak house. The prices aren't cheap, but the meats are mouth-watering. Plenty of options, including the more reasonably priced choices which are now offered. Your best choice in Uptown. 350 Jordan Road. 928-282-7959.

Yavapai Room at Enchantment Resort Over-priced but good, with an exceptional Sunday brunch. Meanwhile, Tii Gavo (their grill) serves one thing best: good views. Reservations are now generally required to enter the property at all, even if you just want to look around. The brunch, by the way, is so good and so big it ought to be outlawed. 525 Boynton Canyon Road. 928-282-2900.

With 10 pizza, pasta, or other Italian establishments, I declare the west side of Highway 89A to be Sedona's "Little Italy." They won't all last, but right now you've got three very good additional choices for this cuisine: **Troia's** (Tu-Sun. 1885 W. Hwy 89A. 282-0123), **Spice's** (2545 W. Hwy. 89A. 928-204-9117), and **Pietro's** (2445 W. Hwy 89A. 928-282-2525), all located along Hwy 89A in West Sedona.

Cowboy Club is your place for the meats of all kinds of critters. You'll want to ask for "The Silver Saddle Room" for fine dining. The atmosphere is definitely Western, and as you pass through the main club room you'll see see jeep drivers in their hats and chaps by the bar, tired from a long day of driving their herds...of tourists. Open daily. Lunch 11am-3pm; dinner 5-11pm. Uptown, 241 N. Hwy 89A. 928-282-4200. www.cowboyclub.com

The Grille at Shadow Rock is more simply known as "The Restaurant at the Hilton" by locals, who know and appreciate Chef Esteban's work. It has received good reviews in its first year of service since the hotel was sold by the Doubletree chain.

Pizza Picazzo, "where pizza is art," is the most successful restaurant opening here in recent history. The reason is that it's not just good, it's addictive. Honestly, from the first bite I thought, "I don't know what they put in this, but I must have more." I stopped to look around and noticed everyone else had the same expression on their faces. No reservations; it's first-come, first-served here. Very reasonable prices in the lively atmosphere of an exceptionally styled building. 1855 W. Hwy 89A. 928-282-4140.

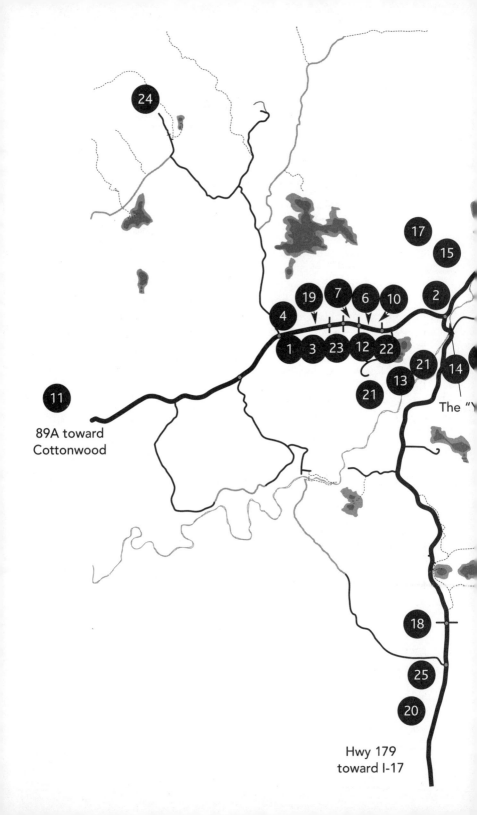

89A toward
Cottonwood

The "Y

Hwy 179
toward I-17

89A toward
Flagstaff

5

1	A Pizza Heaven
2	Cowboy Club
3	Dahl & DiLuca Ristorante Italiano
4	Fournos
5	Garland's Oak Creek Lodge
6	Heartline Café
7	India Palace
8	Javelina Cantina
9	L'Auberge de Sedona
10	Luther's American Bistro
11	Piñon Bistro
12	Pizza Picazzo
13	René at Tlaquepaque
14	Robert's Creekside
15	Savannah
16	Shugrue's Hillside Grill
17	Takashi
18	Tara Thai
19	Thai Spices
20	The Grille at Shadow Rock
21	The Oak Creek Brewery & Grill
22	The Red Planet Diner
23	Troia's
24	Yavapai Room at Enchantment
25	Minami

FUN PLACES, GOOD FOOD

I rate the following eateries on a combination of food and ambience/uniqueness/fun. They're listed below from best to least best according to this index.

Luther's American Bistro is Sedona's newest up-and-coming restaurant. It serves delicious Gulf Coast cuisine and fantastic steaks. Dessert options are cheesecake, cheesecake, or . . . cheesecake. Old Marketplace, 1350 W. Hwy 89A. 928-282-4955. ✚ This close to the border, you have a right to expect good Mexican food. I like **Javelina Cantina** the best. It has a lounge and lively atmosphere to go with the good food. Jessica is the friendliest restaurant manager around and will find you a good spot. Ever have a fish taco? Try one here. Hillside Plaza, 671 Hwy 179. 928-203-9514. ✚ **Minami** in the Village of Oak Creek serves superb sushi and tempura. Affordable too. They may have reopened for lunch as well as dinner by the time you come; if so, don't miss the noon-time noodle specials. Hwy 179, across from Prime Outlets. 928-284-0684. ✚ New for beer lovers is **The Oak Creek Brewery & Grill** at Tlaquepaque. Service and food are average, but the beer is excellent and the decor is well-done and very comfortable. 928-282-3300. ✚ **Tara Thai** has the best Thai food in Sedona, and maybe the best in the Southwest. Located in the Village of Oak Creek. 34 Bell Rock Plaza. 928-284-9167. ✚ **A Pizza Heaven** has won over Sedonans who love pizza, but the pasta is also very good. Here there's a simpler atmosphere, and more outdoor seating, with an occasional musical performer. 2675 W. Hwy 89A. 928-282-0519. ✚ **Fournos** is intimate and unique, serving Greek and Mediterranean food. It offers two nightly seatings. 3000 W Hwy 89A, 928-282-3331. ✚ For fun, eat where the interplanetary visitors eat: **The Red Planet Diner.** A quirky mix of Cajun, Italian, and dinner cuisine in an ambience of crop circle, alien, and Star Trek decor. 1655 W. Hwy 89A. 928-282-6070. ✚ **Thai Spices** is also popular among locals (always a good sign) who like its health-conscious choices. 2986 W. Hwy 89A. 928-282-0599. ✚ Your Uptown sushi alternative is **Takashi,** which has outdoor seating too. Expensive. 465 Jordan Road. 928-282-2334. ✚ **India Palace** is, obviously, Indian. They prepare the meals as mild or as spicy as you like. The buffet is a great bargain. Next to Basha's Plaza, 1910 W. Hwy 89A. 928-204-2300.

EVENTS

S EDONA has lots of events going on throughout the year. Here are the ones that insiders believe are really worth coming to see. I've rated them on a scale of one to five from the point of view of a spectator, with one meaning, "Okay if you happen to be here anyway" and five meaning "Mark the calendar and do what it takes to get here!" If you intend to be a participant, ignore my ratings and go for it! Once you're here, you'll find the *Red Rock Review* is a good information source for exact start times and prices. Meanwhile, New Frontiers Health Food has one of the town's best bulletin boards for smaller events.

February

The Sedona International Film Festival is a marvelous chance for locals and visitors to sample the best of the world's independent productions. The "Sundance of Sedona" is a little festival that has done remarkably well with independent American and foreign movies that won't be showing at the movieplex in your mall. Founded in 1994, it screens 50-60 films. Individual flicks can be viewed for $10 at Harkins Theatres, but day and weekend passes are available. If money is no object, attend the gala event on Friday night, usually held at Enchantment Resort. Someone from Hollywood is sure to be there. Last weekend in February. **928-282-0747. www.sedonafilmfestival.com** ****

March

The **St. Patrick's Day Parade** is held in the Uptown area, typically on the Saturday closest to March 17. It's a fun day when the town in the Red Rocks dresses up green. Look for it on Jordan Road. **928-282-0747.** **½

April

Verde Valley Birding & Nature Festival is full of fun events. Although Dead Horse State Park in Cottonwood is the primary venue, Red Rock State Park and Slide Rock State Park in Sedona also participate. The festival is held on April's final weekend (April 25-27 in 2003) and includes field trips, workshops and of course, bird counts. Over 171 species were seen in 3 days last year. Field trips during the festival weekend have included visiting the Grand Canyon to see condors; viewing birds from the Verde Canyon Railroad train; and "power birding" in Prescott. For information, call Barbie Hart at 928-282-2002 or the special line at Parks and Recreation for the City of Cottonwood, 928-634-8437. **** www.birdyverde.org

The Great Northern Arizona Rubber Duck Race is just as fun and silly as it sounds. Buy a ducky (your raffle ticket) and watch it get dumped with thousands of others into the Oak Creek. First year they all went backwards. Oops! Looks like they've got a better system now. This event is presented by the Sedona Main Street Program and Boys & Girls Clubs of Northern Arizona. Formerly an autumn event, the 2003 event was April 6. 928-204-2390.**

May

On graduation day for students at the **Zaki Gordon Institute for Independent Filmmaking** their final projects are screened at a gala event. This gives you the chance to see the work of students-turned-filmmakers in the intensive two-year program. The best ones are worth seeing. It is usually held on the third weekend in May. 928-649-4265. www.zaki.yc.edu ***

The Phoenix Symphony Orchestra performs at the Georgia Frontiere Performing Arts Pavilion at the Sedona Cultural Park on Memorial Day Weekend. www.sedonaculturalpark.org ***

Sedona Chamber Music Festival offers both American and international performers. Watch for notices of other chamber music events in the spring and autumn. 928-204-2415. www.chambermusicsedona.org ****

Northern Arizona Watercolor Show, sometimes held at Tlaquepaque, is a presentation of the Northern Arizona Watercolor Society. This twice yearly event features the work of up to 20 members. You can meet the artists and purchase original works at this show. May and October, each year. Check with the Sedona Arts Center for information on the society, 928-282-3809, 888-954-4442. www.sedonaartscenter.org. Alternatively, try Tlaquepaque at 336 Hwy 179, 928-282-4838. www.tlaq.com

June

While it may not be summer on the calendar, it certainly is hot enough by the second weekend in June to think of it that way. That's when **Sedona Taste** takes place, a fundraiser for the Boys & Girls Club featuring fantastic food and wine tasting. Fortunately, the shaded grounds give some relief from the heat. Two things are always found at this event: a great time and lots of over-eating. Los Abrigados Resort. 928-282-7822. www.losabrigados.com ***

July and August

Fourth of July festivities hosted by the Lions Club are also held at the Georgia Frontiere Performing Arts Pavilion. The event is fun if you can stand the heat. Fireworks don't usually start till 9 or 10pm. Contact Dr. Serge Wright of the Lions Club, 928-282-4126.**

The best event of the summer is Shakespeare Sedona, which recently included Michael Learner of TV's "The Waltons." The performances are concurrent with an institute dedicated to teaching the Bard to aspiring writers and actors. Performances are now held outdoors at the Sedona Cultural Park, or indoors across the street at Red Rock High School. Performances run from mid-July through early August. 928-282-0747. www.shake-spearesedona.com ***½

The new Sedona Miniature Golf Championship was held for the first time ever at Los Abrigados. Three people who actually make a living doing this flew in for the first event and won all the prize money. Call the spa or concierge desk at Los Abrigados, the championship host. Held in July. 928-282-1777. www.losabrigados.com *

The Sedona Open Golf Championship is now two years old and has both professional and amateur divisions. It is held during the third weekend in July at the Oak Creek Country Club. 690 Blue Rock Boulevard. 928-284-1660. www.sedonaopen.com **

September

Fiesta del Tlaquepaque is a celebration of Mexican culture. It includes food, music, dance, and entertainment on the grounds of the shopping galleria designed to look like a Mexican city. Held on the closest weekend to mid-September. 928-282-4838. www.tlaq.com

Eco-Fest is a music festival promoting education about the ecology. They've had great popular and rock & roll line-ups in the past. They've usually got a great musical line-up with some big names. Adding fun to the event are the booths and vendors. Lately they've added some interesting animals to see as well. Held in mid-September at the Cultural Park. For tickets and information, 800-594-8499. www.sedonaecofest.com ***½

Sedona's biggest, most famous event is Jazz on the Rocks. If you want to come, make reservations now! Recent celebrities included Chuck Mangione. Jazz on the Rocks turned 20 years old in 2001 and moved to the Sedona Cultural

Park. Proceeds benefit music education programs. It begins Friday evening and continues through a Sunday brunch, but Saturday is the big day. It isn't cheap ($55 in advance), so bring a hat for the sun if you plan to sit out there all day. Now held on final weekend in September. Tickets can be purchased at the gate, or call 928-282-1985. www.sedonajazz.com *****

The ancient culture of the Hopi peoples, whose reservation lies several hours north of Sedona, is the highlight of the **Annual Hopi Artists Gathering** in Tlaquepaque. More than 25 Hopi artists present their painting, silverwork, kachina carving and weaving in a two-day show. Demonstrations and dance performances also take place. Held on the final weekend of September. Tlaquepaque, 336 Hwy 179. Contact Art of the Hopi gallery at 928-204-2658. www.tlaq.com ***

October

The **Verde Valley Music Festival** is hosted by Jackson Browne as a benefit concert for the Verde Valley School. Browne usually brings some friends you've heard of, and past performers have included Bonnie Rait and Bruce Hornsby. However, after being held for several years consecutively, the festival did not take place in 2002. Check with the school for future performances. 928-284-1982.***

Sedona Sculpture Walk. The event, now 15 years running, features the work of more than 100 sculptors in a special juried event. In 2002 the walk was moved to the Sedona Cultural Park, giving artists a bit more room to spread out. Held the first week in October and directed by the Sedona Arts Center. Corner of Hwy 89A and Cultural Park Drive. 928-282-3809, 888-954-4442. www.sedonasculpturewalk.com ****

The Sedona Arts Festival is usually held the second weekend in October, and the turnout is immense. Excellent artists from around the country, but the Southwestern focus is naturally the best. Expect every hotel room in town to be booked if you don't call in advance. Sat-Sun 10am-5pm. $5. Red Rock High School field. Corner of Hwy 89A and Upper Red Rock Loop Road, 928-204-9456. http://artsfestival.sedona.net ****

The end of October is the chance for all Sedona's weirdos (I count myself among them) to let out their alter ego in our favorite holiday of the year, **Halloween.** I often wonder if the kids here develop an inferiority complex from seeing how amazingly decked out the adults get! Head to Uptown in costume for the fun. If you want to dress up in style, find out about **Carnaval de Mascaras** at Tlaquepaque. 336 Hwy 179. 928-282-4838. www.tlaq.com ***

December

The **Festival of Lights** is a cherished tradition that involves the lighting of 6,000 luminarias in Tlaquepaque's courtyards and walkways. Performances by carolers, musicians, and dancers take place from noon until dark, with the whole community participating in the lighting at 7pm. Held 12-14 days before Christmas Day. Admission is free. **336 Hwy 179. 928-282-4838. www.tlaq.com**

The **Red Rock Fantasy of Lights** is, let's face it, tacky. However, if you're like me, you'd rather watch other people put up Christmas lights than do it yourself. Add a little hot chocolate, bring some kids, and this can actually be fun.

The opening of the Sedona Cultural Park added significantly to the city's ability to attract famous performers. Acting as a new home for Jazz on the Rocks and Shakespeare Sedona, performers have included B.B. King and Tony Bennett.

I wouldn't drive up from Phoenix for it, but if you're here anyway, drop by. Begins the weekend before Thanksgiving and finishes the weekend after New Year's. **$5 entry. Los Abrigados, 160 Portal Lane. 928-282-1777. www.losabrigados.com** *

OTHER SOURCES FOR INFORMATION:

The Sedona-Oak Creek Chamber of Commerce has an events calendar at **928-282-7722. www.sedonachamber.com**

The **Sedona Arts Center** is worth a visit itself for its member gallery. It also hosts events and exhibits throughout the year in addition to the Sedona Sculpture Walk. **North end of Uptown. 928-282-3809, 888-954-4442.**

The **Sedona Cultural Park** includes the Georgia Frontiere Amphitheatre and the Zaki Gordon Independent Film Institute. **928-282-0747. For event tickets, 928-203-4849, 800-780-2787. www.sedonaculturalpark.org**

Sedona Creative Life Center brings good speakers and seminar leaders to town. **928-282-9300. www.sedonacreativelife.com.**

The Red Rock Review is a monthly publication with a calendar of events, found free of charge all around town. **www.redrockreview.com.**

INSIDE INSIGHT

The Big Splurge, or How to Not Save Money in Sedona

If money is truly no object, then read carefully for the best of the best in town. The first thing you need to do is to make sure you'll be here long enough to spend it. Once your flight plan is set, don't settle for just any rental car. Get yourself a roomy Lincoln Navigator or the sports car of your choice from Resort Rentals in Phoenix. If the money is just burning a hole in your pocket, then have Red Rock Limousines pick you up.

The most important choice will be where to stay. Enchantment Resort in Boyton Canyon on the west side of town is your best bet if you'd like to relax in a gorgeous canyon. But don't settle for just any room in this lavish resort with at least five pools. Ask for Casita 31, the room with its own pool, uphill on the property. Or stay for just a thousand dollars a night at Enchantment's new spa, Mii Amo, and the massage therapist will come to you. If you want something closer to town, try L'Auberge de Sedona. From Cabin 15 you can watch the ducks floating by on Oak Creek as you awake in the morning. However, if first class means "cozy," rely on Sedona's four-diamond bed & breakfasts. Be well treated at Adobe Village, part of the Graham property, located in the Village of Oak Creek.

To spare no expense I'm afraid the jeep and trolley tours aren't pricey enough. Instead, fly above it all with an early morning balloon ride with Red Rock Balloon Adventures. Spectacular! Back on the ground, the chase crew will await your return with a champagne breakfast. To explore more of Sedona once you're on the land, only an exclusive, private guide will do. Steve "Benny" Benedict of Touch the Earth Tours is the choice of discriminating visitors, who enjoy his vast knowledge of every nook and cranny of Red Rock Country, not to mention his warm sense of humor. Tell Benny you want the full private package, and soon you'll be picnicking off the trail at a place so scenic you'll think you are dreaming. For something to serenade you, have him arrange for flutist Jesse Kalu to be there. Unseen in a cavern high above, he'll play music that speaks to your soul.

On your return, indulge yourselves with a "Hot Rocks" massage by Jean Neeley. She'll use the warm basalt stones to channel rich oils through your muscles, loosening every last knot. Mmmm.

So much to spend, so little time! On land, try the new Savannah if you must have the chateaubriand, perhaps the town's most expensive entree. . . and worth it!

It's been a wonderful weekend so far, but with so much more to spend, you may have to divide and conquer. Let one of you play a round at the Sedona Golf Resort, hiring the teaching pro to play 18 with you. The other can hit the shops! There're those cute little sculptures in front of Exposures Gallery, and for a million or so you can have the white sculpture by Francis Jansen. Bring home one of nature's works of art too, with an exquisite quartz crystal from Crystal Magic. Pick up something handmade at Garland's Navajo Rugs to place under your treasures. Now how about for something personal? Visit Garland's sister store in Oak Creek Canyon for exceptional silver jewelry with turquoise and lapis inlays, or visit Geoffrey Roth, Ltd. if you'd like something custom-designed in gold.

When the golfing and shopping are over, take a break for a session with a myofascial massage therapist at Therapy on The Rocks, and do it overlooking Oak Creek. Regroup tonight at Shugrue's Hillside Grill for excellent fare. Or, for the really big splurge, have Arizona Helicopters take you out for "Dinner on the Mesa."

To finish, remember that no Sedona getaway is complete without a dose of esoterica. Try a psychic reading with Zeffi Kefala, who can predict what you'll have to do to pay for all this!

Approximate prices for the big splurge:

Casita 31 at Enchantment	$1,175
Red Rock Balloon Adventure	$300
Private tour	$275
Jesse Kalu	$150
Hot Rocks massage	$125
Dinner at Savannah	$125
James Breski ring from Geoffrey Roth, Ltd.	$17,600
Sedona Golf Resort	$ 92
Exposures sculpture	$1,200,000

Taxes, of course, are not included.

FAMILIES

SEDONA'S overnight visitors are dominated by empty nesters, and that can leave families with kids feeling left out. Here are some options.

LODGING

Try the **Quail Ridge Lodge** whose atypical buildings allow you to fit more people under one roof. The chalets have rooms upstairs and downstairs and face the wilderness area between Castle Rock and Bell Rock. They have a tennis court and pool, too. **120 Canyon Circle Drive. 928-284-9327.** Somewhat more expensive–but still catering to families–are the **Radisson Poco Diablo,** where the "Executive" Golf Course is small enough for big kids **(1736 Hwy 179, 928-282-7333)** and **The Junipine Resort,** with nearby **Slide Rock State Park** and walking trails **(8351 N. Hwy 89A, 928-282-3375).**

THINGS TO DO

Posse Grounds Park includes a play area for children. Kids too small for a big hike? Try a little bitty hike on the little-known **Carruth Trail,** where the names of the plants are posted for educational value. For each, turn north off Hwy 89A onto Posse Grounds Road. You'll see the park first, by bearing left at the signs at the entrance to it. For the trail, continue bearing right and then turn right onto Carruth Road. The trailhead is small, just a few yards up. Park anywhere on the side of the road. **Big Park** has a play area for children by the school. In the Village of Oak Creek, turn west off State Highway 179 onto Verde Valley School Road. The school and park are about a mile from the intersection on the left-hand side of the road. If you need something to put the baby in, **Sedona Sports** rents jogging strollers for babies for $10 per day. They'll loan you a baby backpack for $15 a day and $10 for each additional day. (Rental fee can be used toward the purchase of the pack, if you'd like to take one home.) **Across from Tlaquepaque. 251 Hwy 179. 928-282-1317.**

What this town could use is a good babysitting service! Ask the folks at your lodging and anybody else you can find for a recommendation. The ultra-expensive option is **Enchantment Resort**, whose **Camp Coyote** is perfect for kids. 928-282-2900. If your child doesn't have a trust fund and you happen to be here in the summer, then instead try **Los Abrigados**, which is a kid's best friend with "Leaping Lizards" Monday through Saturday in the summer. This activity program may be the best thing to have happened to Sedona summers. 928-282-1777.

For some **miniature golf**, try the course at **Los Abrigados** where their small course is open until 9pm. $5 for adults, $3 for kids. 160 Portal Lane. 928-282-1777.

The **SuperVue** theater behind the outlet mall in the Village of Oak Creek shows a great movie about Sedona in the huge IMAX format. 6615 Hwy 179. 928-284-3214.

Kids old enough to like amusement park rides will like Sedona's jeep tours. *See "Land Tours" for information on Pink, Red Rock, or Earth Wisdom Jeep Tours.*

KID-FRIENDLY DINING

Desperate for a "Happy Meal"? Our **McDonald's** features the world's only teal green arches in the Safeway Plaza on W. Hwy 89A. For more fun for the kids (and good food for you too), try **Sedona-saurus**, located on Hwy 179 about 1 mile south of the "Y."

Local families also patronize the **Pizza Hut** (with lunch specials) and **Burger King**, 2245 W. Hwy 89A and 166 W. Hwy 89A, respectively.

PARKS

In West Sedona, let the kids work off some energy at **Posse Grounds Park** (turn off Hwy 89A at Posse Grounds Road) or **Sunset Park** (turn off Hwy 89A at Sunset Drive). In the Village of Oak Creek, try the **Kiwanis Bell Rock Playground** next to Oak Creek Country Club (turn west off Hwy 179 at Bell Rock Boulevard).

TOYS

For toys for the kids or grandkids, visit **Sedona Kid Company**, Uptown, 333 N. Hwy 89A, 928-282-3571.

FISHING

The ARIZONA GAME AND FISH SERVICE stocks Oak Creek from the Page Spring Hatchery upstream of the Pine Flat Campground, located high in Oak Creek Canyon. It's pretty simple here: there are brown trout (wild) and rainbows (stocked), but no native trout around. Even if you don't catch a thing, the beauty of Oak Creek makes the visit worthwhile. Some supplies are available from small stores in the canyon, but you're probably better off stocking up in town first.

On The Creek Sedona Outfitters features Orvis products. In addition to rods, gear, and clothing, they offer private guide services on Oak Creek. They have exclusive trespassing rights on some portions of the creek. Rates are typically $135 for a single (one person), and $185 for two; for a full day, it's $185 for a single person and $285 for two people, with lunch and beverages included. More extended day trips to fish at Lee's Ferry in Northern Arizona are available. **Mon-Sat 10am-5pm, Sun 10am-4pm. Uptown, 274 Apple Avenue in between Jordan Road and Hwy 89A. 928-203-9973.**

Sedona Sports has more gear than you might expect and is conveniently located. They offer tackle, bait, and licenses ($12.50 for a one day, non-resident) and rent both spinning and fly rods, with

rates as low as $9 per day. **Open daily. Across from Tlaquepaque, 251 Hwy 179. 928-282-1317. www.sedonasports.com**

Canyon Market. If you're already "up the creek," this market has some bait, flies, and some hooks. **Daily, 8am-5pm. 9440 N. Hwy 89A, (look for Don Hoel's Cabins). 928-282-3560.**

Rainbow Trout Farm provides "everything you will need to hook 'em and cook 'em!" If it's not the sport you want, but just the trout dinner, then consider the farm. Located 4 miles north of Uptown, on the right-hand side. The fish are raised in artesian springs, and the farm features grills and picnic tables. No license required. **Open daily. 3500 N. Hwy 89A. 928-282-5799 or 928-282-3379. artesiansprings@sedona.net**

Licenses are also available in the Village of Oak Creek at **Ace Hardware** (6085 Hwy 179A) and **Webers/IGA** grocery store. On the west side, head to **Rite Aid** (Safeway Plaza, 2350 Hwy 89A) and **Basha's** (Basha's Shopping Center, corner of W Hwy 89A and Coffee Pot Drive).

PRIVATE GUIDE

Years ago a Connecticut fisherman promised that if he ever started his own guide service, he'd call it **Gon' Fishen'**. Voilá. Sedona's only officially licensed guide, Jim McInness knows the fishing holes on Oak Creek as if he grew up here. Jim is licensed for parts of the Verde River as well, but for natural beauty, choose the Oak Creek Canyon.

Half-day outing (4 hours) is $100 for 1 person, $160 for 2. A full day (8 hours) includes a lunch and is $160 for a single, $280 for a duo. Jim will get you a rod for $10 more. Families welcome, but advance notice is needed for groups. To ensure availability, make sure to call ahead in any season except winter. 928-282-0788. Friendly Forest Service personnel have lots of information at the **Oak Creek Visitors Center.** Emmas is a gem. Next to Garland's Trading Post, 3901 N. Hwy 89A, 928-203-0624.

Consider the good book *Arizona Trout Streams and their Hatches,* by Charles R. Meck and John Romher, if you want more details.

The area's first known civilization is now referred to as the Archaic Peoples, though you've probably heard them called the Anasazi. Here are a few good reasons not to use that word anymore. First, it was a Navajo term utilized by a professor trying to find a word that meant "ancestors." "Ancient ones" is what he thought he had come up with. He was wrong. More properly translated, it means "Ancient enemies." Second, there is substantial evidence that these peoples are not related to the Navajo (Diné) people of today.

g

GEOLOGY

THE INTRICATE PROCESS of the elements upon this landscape is a story that speaks in eons of time. Here, we'll break down what has happened in this area into a three-part story. Overly simplified, for sure, but enough to give you the general idea. For a viewpoint from which to see the entire geological story revealed, head up to Airport Mesa as you read this story.

WHY ARE THE ROCKS RED?

The rocks are red because they contain iron, found specifically in minerals like feldspar, quartz, and mica. Why the red is not found elsewhere is hard to say. Geologists now believe that the Schnebly Hill Formation is distinct, and that the processes that laid down its deposits were confined to this area. Travelers who journey further through the Southwest will note that many other places consider themselves to be in Red Rock Country. Look closer though, and you'll see that our orange-red coloring really is unique.

HOW DID IT GET HERE?

Part I of our story begins with the ocean. Everything here was covered by it, approximately 350 million years ago. Ever since, water has moved in and out of the area, usually in progressively smaller quantities. With each successive inland sea, lake, swamp, or stream, new deposits of soil or mud were laid down. In turn, the sand, soil, or mud turned to stone.

You may notice that red stones sparkle in the sunlight like sand on a beach. This is what they once were: dunes of sand which, over the millennia, turned to stone. The "softness" of this rock makes it great for walking on, as it gives you a good grip and is easy on your knees. Most of what you observe in Sedona is this sandstone. Included in this is a layer

900 feet thick known as the bright red Schnebly Hill Formation, not found (or at least not found exposed) at the Grand Canyon or parts north of here.

Part II came more than 200 million years ago, when two tectonic plates (the Pacific and the North American) began moving alongside and into each other. The heavier plate sank, and the lighter plate was lifted above it. The collision created a massive uplift of land known today as the Colorado Plateau. When you understand this point, you'll see that the "mountains" you see in the distance are not mountains at all, but simply the edge of the plateau.

Part III is the least well known chapter of the tale, for few people realize that there are more than 600 volcanoes on the plateau, all of which are inactive today. Between 5 and 15 million years ago, however, they were busy flowing lava. Sedona's House Mountain (located on the south side of town) flowed lava in the area. The dark gray crust seen above the red and white sandstone layers on Wilson Mountain, Sedona's tallest ridge, is basalt, the stone resulting from hardened lava.

Sedona faces substantial challenges in the struggle to balance economic growth, tourism, and the small-town feel that residents hope to preserve. Just as Palm Springs, Boca Raton, and Aspen did in prior decades, so Sedona is fighting to be both accessible and secluded at the same time.

GOLF & TENNIS

I T WAS INEVITABLE that blue skies, yellow sun, and red rocks would be complemented by the green grass of golf courses. While Sedona courses are not in the same league as the more famous Phoenix and Tucson links, you'll never find nicer scenery. Depending on your accommodations, you may have a bit of a drive (in the car), and the farther you drive, the lower your greens fees will be.

PUBLIC GOLF COURSES

Sedona Golf Resort. *Better known to locals as "The Ridge." If you've got a big game and enough wallet to match, play Sedona Golf Resort. This is a course that will challenge you in a setting you won't forget, designed by Gary Panks. Par 71, 6,461 yards. This championship course is lovely and not cheap. The restaurant is nice, too* (928-284-2093). 35 Ridge Trail Drive. 928-284-9355, 877-733-9885. www.sedonagolfresort.com

Rates
Check for updated rates. For the latest year they were as follows.

Dec 2 - Feb 6
$82 Mon-Thu (1-14 days in advance
$92 Fri-Sat (1-14 days in advance)
$69 after 1:00pm

Feb 7 - May 18
$99 7 days a week, 1-14 days in advance
$69 after 2:00pm

May 19 - Aug 28
$82 Mon-Thu, 1-14 days in advance
$92 Fri-Sun, 1-14 days in advance
$69 after 1:00pm

Aug 29 - Nov 30
$99 7 days a week, 1-14 days in advance
$69 after 2:00pm

Dec 1 - Dec 31
$82 Mon-Thu, 1-14 days in advance
$92 Fri-Sun, 1-14 days in advance
$69 after 1:00pm

Discounts
$20 Junior rate when playing with an adult player.

$150 golf card allows you to play for half off any rate. Good for one year.

Rentals

Callaway golf clubs available for $35. Price does not include tax of 6.3%, but does include cart and range balls.

Reservations

Up to 60 days in advance. Tee times are to be guaranteed with a valid credit card number and expiration date. $15 spectator fee for non-playing spectators. 48-hour notice required for cancellations. Reservations for larger groups may be made further in advance. Contact the staff for details at 928-284-9355 or 877-733-9885.

Village of Oak Creek Country Club *is a Robert Trent Jones design that should be next on your list. Now host to the new Sedona Open Golf Championship. Yardage: Black-6,824; Blue-6,353; White-5,965; Red-5,579.* 690 Bell Rock Boulevard. 928-284-1660. www.oakcreekcountryclub.com

Rates

Including golf cart and taxes, per person, for 18 holes:
January-February, $80
March-June, $90
July-September, $80
October-December, $90

Twilight Fees
(Twilight Play begins at 1:30pm)
January-February, $60

March-June, $65
July-September, $60
October-December, $60
Skip the cart and walk for $40 during twilight golf.

9 holes
January-December $50

Reservations

Up to 30 days in advance.
888-703-9489.

Verde Santa Fe. *I like the fact that the word "fe" in Spanish means "faith," which is what I need to play a good round. This is a par 71 that measures 6,404 yards at championship length, 5,917 for regular play, and 4,976 forward. Check out the twilight rate for a great deal.* 1045 S. Verde Santa Fe Parkway, Cornville, AZ. Take Cornville Road exit on Hwy 89A, about 15 miles west heading toward Cottonwood. 928-634-5454.

Rates

With cart: 18 holes
$40 Mon-Thu
$45 Fri-Sun
$25 twilight (after 1:30pm)

With cart: 9 holes
$25 daily

Walking rates: 18 holes
$20 Mon-Thu
$30 Fri-Sun

Sundowner rate
$10 daily, 2 hours before dark, walking only

Junior rates
$10 for 9 or 18 holes

Driving range
$5 large bucket
$3 small bucket
Accepts V, MC, AE, D. Discounts (not valid with any other discounts); the Golf Card, 25% off posted green fee; the PGA Golf Pass, 25% off posted green fee. Reservations up to 7 days in advance for the regular posted rate, up to 3 days in advance for the discounted passes. Lessons $35 per hour. Also available using online registration form.

Canyon Mesa *has a nice little executive course good for a quick afternoon round. It's in the Village of Oak Creek.* $15-$20. 928-284-0036.

The Radisson Poco Diablo (1736 Hwy 179, 282-7333), *is a small "executive" course, but at least it is bigger than* **Enchantment Resort's** *teenyweeny private course, which you miss if you blink.* 928-204-6015.

Beaver Creek *is an 18-holer without the Red Rock views and high prices, located 35 minutes south.* 4105 E. Lakeshore Drive, Lake Montezuma. 928-567-4487.

MINIATURE GOLF

Miniature golf is now available at **Los Abrigados,** and 2002 featured the first ever **Sedona Miniature Golf Tournament,** complete with prize-money and a trio of brothers competing who actually do this for a living. They won. 160 Portal Lane. 928-282-1777.

TENNIS

Tennis is available at **Sedona's public courts,** located on Posse Grounds Drive in West Sedona. Courts have just been completed at the town's new park. Take 89A to Sunset Drive and follow 1 mile toward Airport Mesa. Look for the new park on your right. Visitors can pay to play at **Los Abrigados, Poco Diablo and Sedona Racquet Club.** Enchantment occasionally hosts tournaments open to visitors not staying at the resort.

HEALTH CLUBS

Ridge Spa & Racquet Club, 10 Ridge View Drive, VOC. 928-284-3800.

Sedona Health Club & Spa (a.k.a. Sedona Racquet Club). 100 Racquet Road. 928-282-4197.

Sedona Spa at Los Abrigados, 160 Portal Lane. 928-282-1777.

INSIDE INSIGHT

Grand Canyon

President Theodore Roosevelt once called the Grand Canyon "the place every American should see." With five million visitors a year, it seems we're all trying.

Consider this fact when planning your trip, and you'll realize that there may be ten thousand people coming from the Phoenix and Las Vegas areas to see it too. The good news is that you've got a considerable head start on them, as their trip will take four hours each way.

If you've made Sedona your starting point for a canyon visit, the following route will be less trafficked and more beautiful than the standard approach. See below for recommendations on group tours and the railroad.

I recommend being on your way by nine in the morning with a full tank of gas, leaving Sedona via Hwy 89A through Uptown Sedona into Oak Creek Canyon. Don't believe your map: this route is indeed quicker and lovelier than Interstate 17. Along the way, you'll cross the Midgely Bridge, with a nice look at Wilson Mountain to your left. It is Sedona's highest peak.

Several miles ahead on the left side, you'll see Garland's, the oldest retail store in the area, renowned for its Native American jewelry collection. Seven miles along, you'll pass Slide Rock State Park, the place to beat the heat in the summer. A few miles farther along you'll notice a sign for West Fork, the trail made famous by western novelist Zane Grey in his book *Call of the Canyon.*

Fifteen miles into the trip you rise out of Oak Creek Canyon on severe cutbacks that take you up onto the Colorado Plateau. (A pullover is available on top if you want a better look.) About 25 miles or 45 minutes along (longer if there is traffic), you'll turn right at the sign for Interstate 17 North (Flagstaff) and then left off the overpass to enter the highway. Within a couple of minutes you'll exit to Interstate 40 East, following signs for Albuquerque. On I-40, for perhaps seven miles, watch for signs for Highway 89 and the Grand Canyon. Exit up the ramp, turning left at the light onto another overpass, and turning right as you follow signs for Hwy 89 and "Wupatki."

Hwy 89 takes you through the east side of Flagstaff, passing by the shopping mall and gradually turning north. As you leave the city limits, the speed limits increase. Watch for signs for Sunset Crater Volcano National Monument and Wupatki Ruins. This road forms a semicircle that will eventually bring you back to Hwy 89, farther north. Consider buying a $50 Golden Eagle card here. The card, good for 12 months, will let you in any national park, including Grand Canyon, which will otherwise cost you $20 per vehicle.

I recommend stopping at the visitor centers first at the crater and later at the ruins. A brief walk through the lava fields is enjoyable at Sunset Crater, as is a stop at the ruin sites in the Wupatki area. The volcano erupted nearly one thousand years ago creating, ironically, the conditions for the peoples here to flourish. I like these stops because they give you a feeling of the geographic activity of the region that created the canyon, as well as a sense of the people that lived nearby.

Once you're back onto Hwy 89, turn right to head north. At the intersection with Hwy 64 at Cameron (see signs for Grand Canyon-South Rim), you have your chance to continue directly to the canyon. However, another interesting stop is just a mile further ahead. The famous Cameron Trading Post (past the bridge, on the left) is a Navajo establishment that has the best shopping in the area. There is also food and gas available here. The real treat, however, is to enter the Private Gallery, which most folks don't even realize is here. If you ask politely, the clerk will arrange for you to be escorted upstairs. This is where the real treasures are, including exquisite handmade rugs, pottery, and traditional kachina dolls.

Turning onto Hwy 64 you'll speed along to the less crowded east entrance of the South Rim of the Grand Canyon. There is an interesting overlook along the way at the Little Colorado Scenic View, but by now you may be anxious just to get to the canyon.

Stop here at Desert View, the first viewpoint, and you'll see the Desert View Watchtower, built by architect Mary Colter. Somewhere around here is probably where the first Spaniards saw the canyon in the 16th century. When they did, they estimated the Colorado River to be only six feet wide, so poorly did they grasp the size of the canyon.

The main advantage of this east-side approach is that you'll be able to travel at your own pace, stopping at whichever viewpoints you like. Meanwhile, the crowds on the tour buses from Phoenix and Vegas are crowded around at Grand Canyon Village and forced to take the shuttle system around the west side. I recommend skipping the village, unless of course you want to stay overnight in style. In that case, the choice is El Tovar, with the best view of any lodge in the world. (Other options are lodges in the park, not on the rim, and a couple of hotels in the nearby village of Tusuyan, about six miles outside the main entrance.)

A tiny fraction of the canyon's visitors set foot below the rim, so why not put yourself in an exclusive club? If Bright Angel and South Kaibab—the two best-known and maintained trails—are crowded, consider East Rim trails, which are equally scenic but less well known. Steep but beautiful are Grandview (from the lookout of the same name) and Tanner (which begins at Lipan Point). Remember, you're at a high altitude here, and you feel fine at first because you're going downhill!

You'd think that having seen the IMAX movie 27 times now, the Insider would be sick of it. No way. Located in Tusuyan, along Hwy 64 just south of the canyon, the movie is worth the visit. It plays at 30 minutes past the hour, every hour. Entertaining and educational, it will give you more views from below to go with the ones you've had today from above.

Your final choice is to decide where to end up that night. If you're staying back in Sedona, then the question is whether to stay for sunset (and drive home in the dark), or to head home in the daylight. The newspaper you'll be handed at the entrance gate will list the sunset time for that day as well as some nice places to watch it from. Coming home in the dark, the best route is Hwy 64 (south to Williams, not east to Cameron) to I-40 East. Off I-40, take the "Phoenix/Sedona" exit onto I-17 and then take the exit for Hwy 89A Sedona /Oak Creek Canyon. (If the cutbacks into Oak Creek Canyon really scare you, you can continue south on I-17 to Hwy 179 instead, for a longer but flatter alternative.)

If you don't stay for sunset, I recommend instead that you drive Hwy 64 (south toward Williams, not east to Cameron) and later take Hwy 180 to Flagstaff. This route is just as fast but more scenic, passing the 12,000-foot-high San Francisco Peaks, which may have snow on them. In Flagstaff, follow the signs for Phoenix and I-17 and take the exit for Hwy 89A Sedona/Oak Creek Canyon off the interstate.

If you're heading to Phoenix instead of Sedona, then stay on I-17. If you're going to Las Vegas, take Hwy 64 to I-40 West.

The above route adds 90 minutes or more to your trip, which would otherwise be a two-hour-and-15-minute drive directly from Sedona to the main entrance. However, if you're not interested in anything other than getting to Grand Canyon quickly, the following routes are the most direct.

A) Take I-17 straight into and through Flagstaff. Follow signs for Grand Canyon (Hwy 180), which will take you to the canyon.

B) From I-17 take I-40 West (toward Los Angeles) to Williams, and then go north on Hwy 64 to the canyon. At Grand Canyon Village, check out the Kolb Studio, home of the Kolb brothers, whose black and white photography of the canyon a century ago has stood the test of time. The best place to eat is El Tovar, but reservations are not accepted for lunch.

If you'd like to take a tour to the canyon, Great Ventures is the low-cost mini-bus option. At $95 per person plus tax, the tour includes the Cameron Trading Post, lunch, and the IMAX movie. However, some clients feel that non-stop sound from the guide and the in-vehicle video is too much.

The Grand Canyon Railway is over-rated, for three reasons. First, it doesn't get you there any faster than your car. Second, you see everything. . . except the Grand Canyon! (It leads you through mostly forest and ends short of any views of the rim.) Third, you're stuck once you get there (although the shuttle bus is now an option). Two exceptions that could make the trip worthwhile are (1) if you're going with kids, who will enjoy the staged train robbery or (2) if you're immobile or unable to drive. Don't arrive as early as they recommend; they're trying to get you to buy more stuff before departure. After all, how long does it take to board a train? Do order up a tour once you're at the canyon to enhance the experience.

The train departs Williams at 10:00am, arriving Grand Canyon at 12:15pm. It departs Grand Canyon at 3:30pm, returning at Williams at 5:45pm. Call 1-800-THE-TRAIN (843-8724) for reservations and directions. Classes of service range from coach to luxury observation, with adult tickets running from $54.95 to $139.95 and children's tickets from $24.95 to $109.95. At the canyon, tours range from 90 minutes to 2.5 hours, at $20 to $35 per adult.

For the aerial view, Arizona Helicopter Adventures (928-282-0904, 800-282-5141) and SkyDance Helicopters (928-282-1651, 800-882-1651) each offer a 2.5-hour flight departing from the Sedona Airport. Prices range from $495 to $625 depending on the number of people, and other taxes may apply. If price is no object, the greatest Grand Canyon adventure of all is to go with SkyDance on its "Grand Canyon Havasupai Adventure." This takes you into the canyon to the reservation of the Havasupai people. Here, in an absolute Garden of Eden, you'll find the blue-green waters of Lake Havasu and Mooney Falls, among the most spectacular places on earth. You can even bring your suit and jump in! (Please call for recent schedule changes.)

Much less expensive is the airplane option. Sky Safari Charter &

Air Tours offers you the Grand Canyon for $139 per person. (928-204-5939, 888-TOO-RIDE, www.sedonaairtours.com) Whether flying by plane or by helicopter, note that some companies don't have flying rights over the canyon itself. At Grand Canyon Airport they transfer you to someone else's plane or helicopter: not the preferred option. Double-check with your Sedona-based provider.

If you've waited until you're already at Grand Canyon, then the choice is Papillon Helicopters, from $99 per person (928-638-2419, 800-528-2418) or Air Star Airlines, from $81 per person for 50 minutes (928-638-2139, 800-962-3869). They fly from Grand Canyon Airport, about six miles south of the main entrance.

HIKES

ULTIMATELY, the only tourists who really miss the Sedona experience are those who don't get out into nature. There are dozens, perhaps hundreds, of worthy trails, but I've outlined three of my favorites to get you started. For more choices and details if you'll be here longer, I recommend *Happy Trails: Great Views and Good Feelings on Sedona's Best Hikes*. Written by yours truly.

EASY HIKE

Trail Name: Bell Rock Pathway (VOC)
Elevation Gain: 100 ft.
Roundtrip Time: 1-2 hours

If you're looking for a nice, gentle way to ease yourself into the beauty of Red Rock Country, this is it. First, good signage and a wide path make this trail easy to follow. Second, this trail is a confidence builder, orienting you to a number of things, such as finding your way in Red Rock terrain; setting your limits in high altitude; and remembering how long it actually takes you to walk a mile. All this to be learned. . . and great views, too! Yet even though the trail doesn't wander far from the road, you can have a genuine outdoor experience.

Begin at the Bell Rock Vista Pathway parking lot. The ramada here gives you a few pointers on the area and a decent map is on the side wall. The trail heads east at first, but the views really start as you turn left (north). If Bell Rock were your home, this would be your driveway. To your left you'll notice the Castle Rock pillar and to your right, the impressive Courthouse Butte.

You'll pass trail signs for the "Big Park Loop" and horse riders along the way, but there's no need to be concerned about these. The walk is 1.1 miles to the far side of Bell Rock, and nearly halfway there a small sign will remind you that you're heading in the right direction.

The graded trail begins to turn uphill, but you can handle it.

You've been close to Bell Rock all along, but it isn't until you approach and round its left front side that you might feel like taking a run up onto it. To your right you'll find one avenue to do that, if you like. It is well marked with cairns (the red rock piles wrapped with wire), the local way to mark a trail. So if you'd like to skip up the side of Bell Rock, follow these to any of the plateaus for a sit, a great view, and possible mystical explorations.

If you stay on the trail, great sights greet you as you head east, crossing in front of Bell Rock. The view here is of Lee Mountain, with pointed Gibraltar Rock to the left. Those lucky enough to be here early will see the sun rising above this ridge. In the evening you'll see the red rocks glow orange with the setting sun.

From here your choices are to stay on the main Bell Rock Pathway as it turns left, or to continue ahead and then to the right to walk the Courthouse Butte Loop. Assuming you don't want to wind up 3.5 miles down a 7-mile round-trip route, take the loop. You'll get a bit farther away from the highway and from the Bell Rock crowds this way. You'll also be on a narrower trail and you'll have to pay a little bit closer attention to what's in front of you.

Despite the appearance given by the cairns leading around Bell Rock's side, you can't cut through between Bell and Courthouse. The trail zips up and zags down, winding around the butte. A small but

tempting hillrock is off to your left as you follow the narrowing trail back south and then east, above a creek bed. On one occasion, I walked here when one of Sedona's surprise spring snow storms hit late in April. These storms happen every year, but we all tend to act surprised anyway. In part it is because it is common for the weather to be sunny and 75 degrees the day before and the day after. Anyway, that evening walk brought big wet flakes that quickly melted and drained through here, creating gentle sounds.

The route continues ahead to complete the 2.7 mile loop, leading easily to the wide Bell Rock Pathway.

Directions: From the "Y," head south on 89A for 6 miles toward the Village of Oak Creek. Turn left (east) at the sign for Bell Rock Pathway Vista, just before the Circle K convenience store.

MODERATE HIKE

Trail Name: Brins Mesa
Elevation Gain: 600 ft.
Roundtrip Time: 1.5 -2.5 hours

When I need a trail to have a good long think—or to go a long time without thinking—I hike Brins Mesa. An hour's journey takes you through a pretty canyon to its steep back wall, and then hoists you up on top for your reward. With scenic views and a hearty climb, Brins Mesa is a trail that will take your breath away both physically and emotionally. From the very start, you'll notice the interesting rock formations in the distance to the right (east). The long diagonal one is Ship Rock, and below it is the smokestack of Steamboat Rock. Driving through, the Jim Thompson trailhead will be on the right, and the Cibola Pass start on the left. You'll park at the end of a gravel road, at the site of an old shooting range.

Past the kiosk, the trail climbs a stony section to point you straight at Mitten Ridge, a beautiful hand-shaped formation. You'll continue to rise gradually over the next mile or so. Less than 10 minutes from the start, you'll sense a side path headed left at a point where the trail has a group of stones set like a stair or erosion break into its center. Ignore the path and continue on the main trail, which will soon turn to the right.

Fifteen minutes along, you'll begin to feel as if you are tucked into the canyon. Depending on the portion of the trail, Wilson Mountain

will fill the northern (left) side of this canyon. If you follow along the ridge of Wilson, you may notice a gray layer of rock, distinctly different from the red and blonde sandstone layers below. This layer is basalt, ancient volcanic lava that has hardened, evidence of the amazing complexity of geological activity here.

After 20 minutes of walking, the trail begins to expand to jeep-width. You'll realize that you're not really walking on the canyon floor. To the right, you'll catch glimpses of the floor and begin to feel yourself rising. By now you've got a clear view of the back wall of this canyon, which you are headed toward. Looking at it, you might ask, where's the mesa? It's on top, and you're about to begin the uphill climb to get to it.

Just two minutes ahead, check out the jumbo manzanita trees on the right side of the trail. Most manzanita are two to three feet tall, but these tower over your head. It's also a good marker for the first wrong turn you'll be tempted to make. Just ahead, the trail appears to fork, with either trail looking worth a try. In fact, only the rising left-hand side will get you anywhere. The views and the steepness are about to improve significantly. You are now above 4,500 feet, and this is where the air will begin to feel a little thin if you're not from these parts.

The trail was named for a brindle bull who took refuge here, and you'll need a bull's strength as the uphill staircase leads to the first ridge. As you reach it, the trail turns sharply to the right, heading toward that back canyon wall. Look left and you may notice a rounded red rock edge that makes a nice little viewpoint. It's a good place to take a rest here if you need one.

Climbing higher, the pinon pines and juniper trees cover the canyon floor like a well-made carpet. As you notice an old wire fence to the right, the trail becomes very rocky, requiring as much mental concentration to place your feet as physical effort. You've got another 100 feet to go.

Fast hikers will make it to the mesa in 40 to 50 minutes, while the rest can take as long as 90 minutes. In the spring, the meadow is covered with yellow asters, red persimmons, and orange Indian paintbrush. In the summertime, the meadow is covered with cactus blooms and century plants towering toward the sky. Here the basalt layer of rock over on Wilson Mountain is more obvious as you look to the east. If you head off to the right up along the mesa, the views improve. One hundred feet along the path, Bell Rock becomes visible in the distance.

You've got a few choices now. First, you can continue to stay on the trail, walking over the mesa and heading deeper into the Secret Mountain Wilderness. The complete trail is 3 miles long, ending at a trailhead off a rough dirt road. Unless a car is waiting for you, don't plan on walking all the way there. Second, you can stop and relax here before turning around. Third, you can take an immediate right turn. This choice allows you to soak up more vistas and, if you like, walk another 35 minutes to the edge of the mesa, with splendid views and a real sense of solitude.

Directions: From the "Y," head north on 89A toward Uptown Sedona. At .3 miles, just beyond the first stoplight, use the left lane to turn onto Jordan Road. Follow it directly into the Jordan Park development, and turn left onto Park Ridge Drive. Continue through the cul-de-sac onto the pavement above, which turns to dirt. It's a bit bumpy, but passable for any car. Continue to the end and begin your hike by the kiosk.

DIFFICULT HIKE

Trail Name: Bear Mountain

Elevation Gain: 1,000 ft.

Roundtrip Time: 3.5 -4.5 hours

Bear Mountain offers a big hike with the rewarding views that make the climbing well worth it. It takes concentration, good health and reasonable trail skills though, for there are more than a few opportunities to lose your way. If you expect to reach the top, leave yourself five hours of sunlight, plenty of water, and some food.

Bear Mountain is much bigger than it looks, roughly three times taller than the point you'll believe to be its top. The smart hiker thinks of Bear Mountain in five challenging stages or steps. Each provides a different uphill challenge and a unique reward once you're there. To orient you, note that Bear Mountain lies ahead to the north; you drive in from the east and the road continues to the west. Doe Mesa is behind you, to the south. The easy start drops through a pair of washes to bring

you to the sign-in table. Given the challenge ahead, it makes good sense to add your name and start time to the list.

To the First Step:

For a couple of weeks each spring, this first portion is a massive, luxurious bed of purple owl's clover. The rest of the year, it is a mere prelude to the coming climb, a chance to make sure this is really what you want to do today. The path begins to rise, with the main zig heading right to bring you to the foot of the cliff. You'll probably be walking about 10 minutes when you come upon a cave-like indentation in the sandstone wall. Make sure to turn left as you head up through the first chute. This brings you up above the step, though you still need to walk uphill following small cairns. This is a constant feature of Bear Mountain: even when you've reached a step, there's higher to go.

A trail of rocks usually signifies a boundary, so a few rocks in a row does not necessarily mean "follow us this way," but more likely "Don't head this way." Meanwhile, on Bear Mountain most cairns (which are for following) are low, and in a recent climb I was surprised to see more than a few had fallen.

To the Second Step:

It's a further 10 minutes on the trail as it slowly moves into the red bowl of rock that forms a beautiful backdrop. Early on, you'll pass a large boulder on the right as your western turn becomes obvious. Farther up, make very sure to cross the dry creek bed that cuts the trail. Unlucky hikers tend to turn here, and not long ago it was full of cairns suggesting that was what you should do. Instead, you'll see a cairn on the other side of the path, which continues along toward the red rocks, but at an angle.

Surveying the red rock walls, it is nearly impossible to tell where or how you'll be getting up. Just wait. The trail will climb up and step down a bit more vigorously, until eventually the trail decides you're ready for an uphill stretch. It's a strenuous but enjoyable uphill, leading eventually to another chute penetrating the red rocks.

Like the first step, even when you're there, you're not yet done with the uphill. The key here is to pay attention to the trail. Where below it cut through manzanita, here the low brush doesn't distinguish the main trail from others. Heading forward (north), skip the temptation to turn left (west) for a distant view, or right to walk along the step's flatter portions.

Moving on to the ridge of the second step, you still need to be attentive. Again, side trails tempt you to scoot up to the left and right for views. Generally, however, your path moves over and across the hill, eventually curving down leftward on the backside. Take a peek at the next saddle, but remember to head back to the main trail exactly as you stepped away from it.

To the Third Step:

The key here is that you aren't so much worried about getting to the top of this step. Instead, you are trying to get across it, bypassing its highest point. Heading down and around the backside, around to the right, you'll eventually reach the next saddle. Once again, the trail is leading you to a west-facing viewpoint, this one among the most dramatic.

To the Fourth Step:

This is the toughest climb of the journey. For one thing, you are higher up. To me, it looks like stones with a hair net on. Thin black lines of moss coat the ridges and ripples of sandy stone. Pause to look for the small cairns, leading across and then uphill. Fantastic views into Fay Canyon appear behind you.

The Big Finish:

The final portion of the trail is steep, but rewarding. The trail is less obvious here, alternately heading over sandstone and through low manzanita. The key turn comes as the trail reaches a steep stone slope. Here you'll turn left and begin a traverse across Bear Mountain. Like a chess piece moving forward, it's a few steps up and a few steps over.

At the Top:

A surprise is ahead. Follow the narrow trail forward to a fallen log. Cross it and you'll come to the cliff edge. The first surprise is down below, where the Palatki ruins mark years of Sinagua habitation. The second is to the north, where the snow-capped peaks of Flagstaff loom. At 12,000 feet, they are the highest in Arizona and they are impressive. The San Francisco Peaks are sacred to the Navajo, and Bear Mountain is one of the few trails that give you a view of these mountains from Sedona. Congratulations! Return route is the same way back.

Driving directions:
From the "Y," take Hwy 89A west for over 3 miles, turning left at the stoplight onto Dry Creek Road. Head 2.9 miles on Dry Creek Road, turning left and following signs for Enchantment, Boynton Pass, and

Palatki. Follow 1.6 miles to the stop sign and turn left onto 152C, the dirt road. It's 1.2 bumpy miles to the parking lot, but a 4-wheel drive is not necessary if you drive gently.

SUPPLIES

Sedona Sports won't let you get outdoors unprepared. First, they're excellent at finding the right hiking shoes for you. Second, they've got all possible accessories, from hats to socks, walking sticks to hydration packs. Across from Tlaquepaque, 251 Hwy 179. 928-282-1317.

Canyon Outfitters has a good selection of hiking boots, as well as plenty of trail maps and information. Climbing is a strength of the store: the staff has considerable experience, and the store carries carabiners and climbing books. West side of town, 2701 W. Hwy 89A. 928-282-5293.

to
Flags

Bear Mountain

Brins Mesa

the "Y"

89A / Oak Creek

89A | West Sedona

to
Cottonwood
and Jerome

TIPS FOR HIKERS

1. Bring plenty of water and stay hydrated. You can lose as
   much as a liter an hour if exercising, and symptoms of
   dehydration set in quickly. Experts recommend cold water
   rather than warm and sipping rather than "chugging."

2. Stick to marked trails. Small rock piles called "cairns"
   (ka-rens) are your guides in Red Rock Country.

3. Sign in at the trailhead. Even better, tell somebody in town
   where you're headed and when you'll return. Don't count
   on your cell phone; most don't work in Sedona's wilderness
   areas.

4. Consider hiking poles, perhaps the simplest way to
   increase stability and reduce strain on your knees.

5. Wear sunscreen, and consider a shady hat on hot days.

Bell Rock
Pathway

Highway 179

to I-17

HORSEBACK RIDING

Y ou've come to the Old West, so why not go for a horse-back ride, pard'ner? Against the backdrop of Sedona, this is your chance to make your cowboy or cowgirl fantasies come true. I recommend a ride because you'll have great views and an enjoyable time. The downside of these rides is that if you're an experienced rider looking to gallop, you won't enjoy the slow pace of a group ride. Meanwhile, consider the jeep ride to the ranch seriously. While there is some touring, the focus is really on getting you to the ranch. I would not consider it a good substitute for a full, traditional jeep tour, but it's perfect if you just want a taste. Check with the tour operator for your pick-up, which may be in Uptown or at your hotel. In the latter case, realize that if they are picking you up (very convenient), they may be picking up others too (not so convenient!). Note that ride times change with the season. Finally, be aware of the physical requirements for riders, so that you or your compadres aren't too young, too short, or too wide by the ranch's standards.

Trailhorse Adventures operates out of the former Kachina Stables and is the best choice if you'd like to go horseback riding alone or want a glimpse of Oak Creek and Cathedral Rock. There are 1-hour ($30 pp + tax) and 2-hour ($50 pp + tax) rides throughout the day. I recommend the latter, which is substantially more scenic. Add lunch or dinner onto a ride and pay a total of $75 plus tax. Early risers can try the breakfast ride for $60. For something longer, there is a half-day ride for $90. For $75 plus tax, a Red Rock Jeep will bring you from Uptown or your hotel and take a different route to get you to the 2-hour horseback ride, for a 3.5 hour total. (Uptown, 928-282-6826. www.redrockjeep.com) To get there on your own, take 89A west for about 5 miles from the "Y," turn left on Lower Red Rock Loop, go 1 mile and turn right onto Elmerville, go .5 mile, then turn right onto Mockingbird Lane. The ranch is an eighth mile ahead. 928-282-7252. www.trail-horseadventures.com

A Day in the West is based at the Bradshaw Ranch, homesteaded 100 years ago, and site of a genuine Western movie set. This is the best feature of the ranch: it's far from civilization, has lots of character, and shows off broad scenic vistas. Of course, it takes longer to get there, so the 1-hour ride on the horse ($55 pp) is combined with a jeep ride there and back for a 3-hour total. I recommend the "Complete Western Experience" if you want a bigger adventure. It's great for families too. This includes the ride there, a 25-minute jeep adventure, an hour-long trail ride, and a dinner back at the ranch. Cost is $99 plus tax per adult, $79 plus tax per child. In addition to rides, they also handle private parties and cookouts. Private rides are pricey, since you'll be paying for the jeep too. At $120 per hour (1-4 people), a 2-hour trail ride with tax is $525.12. However, breaking that down among 4 people, it works out to about $131 per person. Located next to Orchards restaurant in Uptown. **928-282-4320, 800-973-3662. www.adayinthewest.com**

M Diamond Ranch may be a better alternative if you are a highly experienced rider who wants something private. For shorter or less challenging rides, however, I wouldn't recommend them, since the ranch is 20-25 minutes away in the town of Rimrock, which lacks the red rock splendor of Sedona. It is interesting out there, though, because M Diamond is a genuine working cattle ranch.

Now here's something fun: get 5 city slicker friends and join them for a genuine cattle drive ($100 pp plus tax, 48 hours' advance notice). Their prices start at $49 plus tax for 1 hour, and $59 plus tax for 2 hours. Given that they are off the beaten path, you may get your private adventure for the price of the group. **Rimrock, AZ. 928-592-0148. www.mdiamondranch.com**

For a great look at the lives of settlers in Sedona, visit the Sedona Heritage Museum, in Uptown. Jordan Road, 928-282-7038.

ICE CREAM

ITH SUN COMES FUN, and around here, that means ice cream. Here are the best choices, divided by neighborhood.

Black Cow Cafe is my all-time favorite. Start running now, so you're not at the back of the line. They offer a coffee bar, both ice cream and frozen yogurt, juices, draft root beer, and lunch specials. 229 N. Hwy 89A. 928-203-9868.

The largest and closest Native American group in the area is the reservation of the Yavapai-Apache Nation. Originally two separate cultures, they were sequestered together by the U.S. Cavalry at Fort Verde. Today the reservation is by the town of Camp Verde, by the ruins of Montezuma Castle and the Cliff Castle Casino.

Sedona Delights Ice Cream & Frozen Yogurt Shoppe is nearby, across the street. 276-C N. Hwy 89A. 928-282-1785.

Sedona Ice Cream Parlour & Sandwich Shop has been in Sedona a long time now. Consider them for a sandwich to take on your hike. Village of Oak Creek, IGA Shopping Center. 100 Verde Valley School Road. 928-284-5912.

Dairy Queen tastes just as good as it did when you were a kid. You'll find it in Oak Creek Canyon. 4551 N. Hwy 89A. 928-282-2789.

INDIAN RUINS

Y OU MAY HAVE COME FOR THE RED ROCKS, but you should stay for the archeology. Truly, these places will enrich your visit. Let's have a hand for the "Friends of the Forest" and the Verde Valley Archaeological Society. These groups often provide volunteers who can give more information about what you're seeing. I list the major sites here and my recommendations on which to visit below.

The first three sites are U.S. Forest Service controlled and are accessible via the Red Rock Pass. (*See "Parks & Passes" for details.*) The latter three are all in the domain of the National Park Service.

Unfortunately, **Palatki** and **Honanki** are in the opposite direction from V—V (pronounced "V Bar V"), Montezuma Well, and Montezuma Castle. So here are my recommendations. First, if you have the time, visit the ruins and rock art at Palatki, especially if you are in Uptown or West Sedona. From the Village of Oak Creek, the V-Bar-V Ranch is closer, but double-check that the site is open on your date of interest. There are no ruins here but the rock art is awesome. Each involves direct roads that are graded, so passenger cars can handle them. You won't be disappointed, although you may be dusty. If you are at V-Bar-V and time permits, check out nearby Montezuma Well.

If you have problems walking or if you have little time, visit **Montezuma Castle.** If time is a concern, these ruins are a nice option on the way back to Phoenix.

V-Bar-V Ranch is a place that boggles me every time I see it. Imagine nearly a thousand petroglyph images drawn or etched over just a couple of rock walls. Please note the limited schedule. They are open weekends, and often Fridays and Mondays as well. If you like ancient rock art, this is it! Follow Hwy 179 south under the I-17 overpass. Watch for signs for the site several miles ahead, to the right. Entrance with Red Rock Pass ($5 day pass per vehicle). Hours are currently Friday through Monday, 9:30am-4:30pm, but note that the entry gate closes at 3:30pm. U.S. Forest Service, Sedona/Beaver Creek Ranger District, 928-282-4119. www.redrockcountry.org An interesting unofficial website is aztec.asu.edu/aznha/vbarv/vbarv.html

Palatki is one of Sedona's special secrets. I like it because you can find petroglyphs stretching back 6000 years as well as wonderful ruins here. Great photos can be taken of both, particularly the ruins, which are set within a sheltering red rock cliff. About 25-30 minutes from Uptown, on dusty but passable dirt roads. Take Hwy 89A 9 miles southwest of Sedona to Forest Road 525. Follow the signs north for 6 miles. Take Forest Road 795 for 1.5 miles to the entrance gate. You can return via FR 152 to Boynton Canyon Road, then Dry Creek Road to Hwy 89A. Daily, 9:30-4:30pm, but gate closes at 4pm (so the Ranger can drive home to Flagstaff?). U.S. Forest Service, Sedona/Beaver Creek Ranger District, 928-282-4119. Closed New Year's Day, Christmas Eve and Christmas Day, Thanksgiving, and often during bad weather. (So don't trust signs that say "Open Every Day"!) www.redrockcountry.org Again, for more information, visit aztec.asu.edu/aznha/palatki/palatki.html

Honanki contains more extensive ruins, but oh, the price your car will pay to get you there. The petroglyphs are a bit less accessible and are considered less varied. I send folks there who want a more unique experience and who are willing to put their car through anything. Near to Palatki as the crow flies, but far away as the car drives. If you do make it, you'll generally have it to yourself (per Forest Service, you should be out by dusk). Note that reconstruction work is in progress there. Take Hwy 89A southwest of Sedona to Forest Road 525. U.S. Forest Service, Sedona/Beaver Creek Ranger District, 928-282-4119. Currently, their website does not mention Honanki. Good information is at aztec.asu.edu/aznha/palatki/honanki.html

Montezuma Castle is neither a castle nor connected to Montezuma, but don't let a bad name keep you from seeing a great spot. Of all the ruins here, it's the only one you may have heard of before arriving. These ruins are set up high, tucked into the cliffside. Below these ancient condos are a self-guided walking tour, bookstore, and rangers available for questions. 30 minutes from Uptown Sedona, 22 minutes from the Village of Oak Creek.

Directions: Take Exit 293 from I-17 and drive 4 miles on passable gravel/dirt roads. **8-5 daily. National Park Service, 928-567-3322. $3 per adult, 16 and younger free. www.nps.gov/moca/home.htm**

Montezuma Well is interesting in different ways, since it served as the water source of the agriculture for the peoples of this area. 11 miles from Montezuma Castle. No entrance fee is charged. Visitors walk a .3-mile loop trail to see the limestone sink, through which a million and a half gallons of water flow each day. Prehistoric Hohokam and Sinaguan cultures took advantage of this source of water by irrigating crops of corn, beans, squash, and cotton. Makes a nice combination visit with Montezuma Castle and V-Bar-V. 30 minutes from Uptown Sedona, 22 minutes from the Village of Oak Creek. Directions: Take Exit 293 from I-17 and drive 4 miles on passable gravel/dirt roads. **Free entry. Call National Park Service for opening hours, 928-567-4521. www.nps.gov/moca/well.htm**

Tuzigoot is the name for a pueblo built on a hillside by the Sinagua, probably around A.D. 1000. While most of the remains lack tall walls or a ceiling, the views go on for miles. Follow Hwy 89A west for 20 miles through Cottonwood toward Clarkdale, following signs for "Tuzigoot National Monument." 30 minutes from Uptown Sedona. **Open Daily. Summer: 8am-7pm; Winter: 8am-5pm. Closed on Christmas Day. $3 per adult, 16 and younger free. National Park Service, 928-634-5564, www.nps.gov/tuzi/home.htm**

The arriving Spaniards in this region found remains of an already departed people and named them the Sinagua, from Spanish *sin*, meaning "without" and *agua*, meaning "water." This referred to the dry farming techniques the people had apparently used.

JEROME

THE MOST INTERESTING NEARBY TOWN to Sedona must be Jerome. By the early 1900s, it was the center of action in these parts, home of a rich copper mine, several saloons, and at least as many brothels. Jerome gets its name from Eugene Murray Jerome, a New York financier who invested in the mines but never even visited the town.

Jerome makes a fun side trip if you have more than a weekend in the area. Given the size of the town, you can find any place easily.

In 1929 **Jerome's** population reached a staggering 15,000 people, many of whom helped it become one of the world's wealthiest mining sites. After the stock market crash though, the price of copper dropped through the floor. By 1932 the United Verde Mine closed and Jerome became a ghost town. In 1967 the town was registered as a National Historic Landmark, but it remained a ghost town for years, until the 1970s when it became a hippie haven. In 1979 the entire town was arrested, including the mayor, for growing . . . let's call it "an illegal agricultural product." The 1980s and 1990s saw an influx of artists and art retailers. Today, it is home to about 500 people. The **Mine Museum** is interesting and you can toss a coin into the Sliding Jail for kicks. I like the **Haunted Hamburger** as a place to grab some good food. Aim for the second floor to get superior views or try the **Flat Iron Cafe. The Grand Hotel** is further up the block and has a renovated restaurant. The **Gold King Mine** is slightly out of the way, 1 mile to the north. Look for signs, and don't be surprised if you see one that says "Haynes, Arizona." This was once considered a separate town. There are old cars, old tractors, and old mules to see. What will attract you most in Jerome is the interesting arts and crafts of the town. Among other spots, try **Nellie Bly**, a shop that features wonderful kaleidoscopes and periodic art demonstrations. Ask about the bygone brothels of the neighborhood's past. **The Spirit Room** is a saloon that acts as Fun Central in Jerome, located on the one and only street in town, and the place to park your Harley. No kidding: the town becomes Hog Heaven on the weekend, when motorcyclists cruising through the Southwest drop in to hear the hippie band play.

INSIDE INSIGHT

Saving Money in Sedona

In a low-priced state, you've entered an island of price inflation. It takes a special effort and some inside information to find ways to save money around here. The good news is that Sedona's best asset—the views—is free!

Your least expensive sleep options got a little costlier when the Forest Service began limiting where you can pitch a tent outdoors. Unless you are prepared to hike a couple of miles into the forest, you are restricted to official campsites throughout Oak Creek Canyon. The cost is $15 per night. *(See "Camping" for details.)*

The cheapest place indoors is certainly Hostel Sedona. Located on the corner of Brewer and Ranger Roads, you can find it by turning at the Burger King on Hwy 89A by the "Y," and following for one block until you see the building with the Christmas lights. They charge $15 per night for a bunk bed with your own bed sheet/sleeping bag in their dormitory, or $20 if they provide the linens. If you pay the $90 up front for six nights, your seventh night is free. A private room is available for $30 per night for a single, $35 for two. They don't allow tents, pets, or children under 16. Payment is accepted in cash or traveler's checks with valid ID.

If you can't part with your pets, or can afford a little more, then try the White House Inn, which is usually $40-$50 per night for a couple.

If you're willing to spend a bit more, Sky Ranch Lodge is the best value in town. Rates are around $80 per night, but take a few steps to the Airport Mesa overlook and there is all of Sedona in its glory. A hot tub and nice gardens are a bonus. Note that room taxes in Sedona are substantial and will up the price of all these accommodations.

I wouldn't call it "cheap," but there are great bargains to be had at the nicer places in town during the off-season. In winter and summer, rates go down everywhere, from the moderate Kokopelli Suites to the luxurious Enchantment Resort. Call for prices.

Because some have abused the privilege, nearly all coffee houses in town have rules against taking three hours to drink your one single cup of java. But buy your daily caffeine at Brew at the View in Uptown and you can go outside and watch the tourists and the mountains all day long. Bagels are a cheap way to fill up: try New York Bagels in West Sedona. For a bigger breakfast, try the economical Cafe & Salad Company in the Safeway Plaza.

For lunch, begin by plunking down 50 cents for the Friday edition of the *Red Rocks News,* or just check around for a free copy. In *The Scene* weekend section you'll find coupons for India Palace and other local restaurants. While the sandwiches are not particularly cheap at Sedona Memories, they're big enough to cover lunch and dinner. Call in advance and get a free cookie with your order!

For dinner, the Hideaway serves good, reasonably priced Italian food, even less expensive with their 20% VIP card. You can pick one up at the Chamber of Commerce, Uptown at 331 Forest Road, 928-282-7722. Use it to try the Hideaway's veggie lasagna. They are located just below the "Y" on Hwy 179. While you're at the Chamber, ask for the Sedona Superpass. It's filled with hundreds of coupons for local meals, attractions, and shopping.

When is an appetizer a meal? When it is a salad at Robert's Creekside Grill. If you want to dine with the chic but not pay the price, make this your budget splurge meal. Located in the Creekside Plaza, just south of the "Y" and not far past the Hideaway. If your small budget and great big appetite come into conflict, then try for Joey Bistro at Los Abrigados mid-week. Wednesday is All-You-Can-Eat Crab Legs. Thursday is All-You-Can-Eat Pasta. In Los Abrigados Resort, also just south of the "Y."

The good news is that the hiking is free, although the Forest Service now asks that you pay for parking. (*See "Hikes" for details.*) Absolutely free is the beautiful Chapel of the Holy Cross, located on Chapel Road, off Hwy 179 north of Bell Rock. It's free of charge, not free of tourists. From here you'll see Bell Rock, Cathedral Rock, Courthouse Butte, and the Lee Mountain formation. To get the views that the tour companies offer, visit Airport Mesa. To be by the creek without paying for it, stop at Indian Gardens in Oak Creek Canyon. Or, you can drive north past Slide Rock State Park, squeeze into a safe parking spot on the left side of 89A, and shimmy down to the water for free. Rangers don't mind, but be careful to stay off the narrow road.

What about free entertainment? Jesse Kalu plays on Saturday and Sunday evenings without charge for some wonderful musical entertainment. (He does accept donations though, and you should consider offering one.) See him at Sedona Pines Resort and at the Sedona Heart Center.

Want the spa experience without paying resort prices? Visit the Arizona Healing Center where you can take a sauna for just $7. The hot tub is $10 per person and a session in the flotation tank is $60.

Can't afford to pay a week's salary for a round at the Sedona Golf Resort in the high season? Think small, and try the miniature golf course at Los Abrigados for $5 per person. For some low-cost history lessons, visit the Sedona Heritage Museum.

There's one last way to try some activities in town: sign on for a timeshare tour. Note that they'll try to prequalify you by inquiring about your annual income. If it's not above $25,000 or so per year, you won't get the deal. And what is the deal? Usually it is a free jeep or biplane tour, a free meal, or a discounted stay at a local accommodation. Realize, however, that you're committed to 90 minutes of mental anguish. If they don't succeed in weakening your defenses against buying, then they'll probably succeed in making you feel horribly guilty that you took the tour when you were never really interested.

To sum it up, here's the cheapest sleep: Hostel Sedona, 5 Soldiers Wash Drive, 928-282-2772; White House Inn, W. Hwy 89A, 928-282-6680; Sky Ranch Lodge, Airport Road, 928-282-6400; Kokopelli Suites, 3119 W. Hwy 89A, 928-204-1146.

Here are the cheapest eats: New York Bagels, 1650 W. Hwy 89A, 928-204-1242; India Palace, adjacent to the Basha's Shopping Center, 1910 W. Hwy 89A, 928-204-2300; Cafe & Salad Company, in the Safeway Plaza, 2370 W. Hwy 89A, 928-282-0299; Sedona Memories, 321 Jordan Road, 928-282-0032; Hideaway, just below the "Y" on Hwy 179, 928-282-4204; Robert's Creekside Grill, in the Creekside Plaza just south of the "Y"; and Joey Bistro, at Los Abrigados Resort, 160 Portal Lane, 928-282-1777.

Here are some good things that are absolutely free: Chapel of the Holy Cross, off Hwy 179, 4 miles south of the "Y" (turn left onto Chapel Road); Airport Mesa (follow 89A 1.1 miles west from the "Y," then turn left onto Airport Road); Indian Gardens (north on 89A, look for Garland's); and Slide Rock State Park, off Hwy 89A, 7 miles north of Uptown.

Jesse Kalu plays at Sedona Pines Resort (6071 W. Hwy 89A, 928-282-6640). Arizona Healing Center is located in Uptown, but directions are tricky. It's best to call them at 928-282-7710.

Lastly, here are a few details about what's next to free: Los Abrigados golf costs $5 per person. Sedona Heritage Museum costs $3 per person (those under 12 enter free); open daily 11am-3pm except for major holidays, 735 Jordan Road, 928-282-7038.

Timeshare tours are available with Fairfield (2445 W. Hwy 89A, 928-203-9744), Sedona Vacations/ILX (Los Abrigados et al., 928-282-2394), Sunterra (Sales Office at 55 Sunridge Circle, 928-284-0689), Sedona Pines (6071 W. Hwy 89A, 928-282-6640). Got too little money to call them? Then just enter the suspicious-looking "Activity Center" or "Tourist Information Booth." Don't even want to walk that far? Don't worry: stand around outside long enough and they'll find you.

Sedona

FOUNDED 1902

1

LAND TOURS

JEEP TOURS

Jeep Tours are the most popular way to see the sights if your time is short and you can't or don't want to walk the land yourself. Since Sedona is a transient town, one drawback is that your driver may have arrived in Sedona just shortly before you! So ask which trail the most experienced driver is taking today to get the most knowledgeable guidance.

If the weather has been dry, I'd advise sitting in the front of the jeep, or in the front jeep if more than one is going out. Otherwise, you'll be eating a dust sandwich for lunch. Note that some listed prices require a minimum number of people in the jeep.

Could you get to these places by yourself? In some cases, you could. However, considering the time it would take you to find them on your own—not to mention the damage to your car—these tours are a good way to see a lot of Sedona, and far more informative.

Pink Jeeps is the reigning king of the jeeps. I rate "Broken Arrow" as best, as it passes through the beautiful red formations where Jimmy Stewart starred in the Western of the same name. If you have a little more time and the interest, then seriously consider "Ancient Expeditions," which will take you to see petroglyphs and ruins both at Honanki and on some private land. Take any tour you can with Mike Peach, Sedona historian. **$35-$90 per person. Located at the south end of Uptown, by the traffic light. 928-282-5000, 800-873-3662. www.pinkjeeptours.com**

Red Rock Jeep Tours are no less fun. Best is "Soldier's Pass" (1.5 hours, $49) which visits several dramatic geologic formations. They recommend "Canyons & Cowboys," which takes you further into the wilderness for sunsets. (1.5 hours, $36, 2 hours, $44). Old Bear Wallow takes you up the Schnebly Hill Road for the most scenic vistas. (1.5-3 hours, $36-$64). All prices per person, plus tax. Other tours also available. **Located in Uptown on the east side of the street, between the two stoplights on the south end. 928-282-6826, 800-848-7728. www.redrockjeep.com**

Earth Wisdom Tours are in jeeps too, but it isn't the bouncing around that's the focus. Instead, it is on the spirituality of the area, including the Native American perspective. If you have an interest in Sedona's mystical vortex energy, or you'd like to get out and walk the land a bit, Earth Wisdom is the best among jeep companies. Tours from 2-4 hours, $42-$68 per person. In the middle of Uptown in the Rollie's Camera courtyard. 928-282-4714, 800-482-4714, www.SedonaTraveler.com.

The Adventure Company has 1-hour and 2-hour jeep tours departing from the Tlaquepaque shopping area. Their scheduling is less "on the hour" than the others, and they can often leave once you show up (assuming there is more than one of "you"). 1-hour tours average $35 per person for a full jeep; 2-hour tours are $50 per person. 877-281-6622. www.sedonajeeptours.com

See Car Rentals" if you'd like to rent a Jeep for yourself.

OTHER SEDONA TOUR OPTIONS

Way of the Ancients offers tours within Sedona and beyond to the Grand Canyon, the Hopi Mesas, and other famous places in Arizona. "Sedona Sacred" is a 5-hour tour of the Verde Valley. $75 per person, with a minimum of 4 people. 465 Jordan Road, Suite 2. 928-204-9243. www.sedonasacred.com

A Hummer Affair is clearly the macho choice, taking you in a Swiss-made Hummer vehicle. You'll get bigger bumps but no less safety, since you'll be strapped in like a fighter pilot. Most tours are 1.5-2 hours and $79-$110 per person. A unique offering is the "Historic Jerome" tour, which visits wild country on the way to the old ghost town of Jerome. 5 hours: $225.00/person with 2-3 people; $125.00/person with 4-8 people. Tour office is Uptown on the west side of the street; tours depart from Sedona Sports, 251 Hwy 179, across from Tlaquepaque. 928-282-6656. www.hummeraffair.com

The Sedona Trolley gives you the chance to see Sedona on either of two 55-minute tours starting from the Cheers store across from the Chamber of Commerce Visitor Center in Uptown. This is the exact opposite of what the jeeps and Hummers offer: a gentle ride and low prices. Although I run the other way when I see it coming (it screams, "Hordes of Tourists Arriving!"), I must admit that at $8 per adult, $3 per child, it's a pretty good value. Tours depart every hour on the hour, 7 days a week, starting at 10am. The three trolley cars can also be chartered for special events. 928-282-5400. www.sedonatrolley.com

Tara Golden of Wet Paint Studio offers art tours in Sedona. During the tour, Tara brings you to the workshops of up to 3 local artists, to understand their creative process. In some cases, stops at Sedona galleries are included. 3 hours, $75 per person. 928-203-4156. www.sedonaarttours.com

PRIVATE GUIDES

Although each individual below has a distinct company name, the truth is that we're talking about private guides here. Each is a one-person show, generally speaking. Many fly-by-night guides try to make a living doing this in Sedona: those who I've listed are the ones who are committed to stay and know their stuff.

Steve Benedict of **Touch the Earth Tours**, a former ranger, has the most substantial background in nature guiding among those listed. "Benny," as he is known to clients, takes a very down-to-earth approach that isn't so less geared toward explaining what's going on, and more focused on showing it to you. 928-203-9132. www.earthtours.com

Sandra Cosentino of **Crossing Worlds Journeys** offers private tours focused on vortexes and medicine wheels as well as extended journeys to the Hopi Mesas. 928-203-0024. www.crossingworlds.com

Suzanne McMillan McTavish is a long-time Sedona resident (around here that means more than 5 years) offering group outings. It's not easy to find guides with an office and an established center. Look for her at Sedona Heart Center next to the Highway Café. 1405 W. Hwy 89A. 928-282-2733. www.sedonaretreats.com

Rahelio of **Sedona Mystic Tours** caters to the most esoteric crowd. But let's be honest: despite what you've heard or what's been suggested, he's not Native American. He does, however, know much about Indian traditions, and he offers some nice ceremonies. For a shaman-with-a-drum, this is your man. www.rahelio.com

Finally, consider Meta Adventures with **Dennis Andres**. I tend to work best with those who want a well-rounded journey into nature. I include a discussion of how the red rocks came to be, the Native American story of this area, and extensive information on plant and animal life. The hiking is as gentle or as vigorous as you desire. For those who desire it, I lead a meditation to help you make a deeper connection with Sedona's nature and energy. It gets great reviews. Best for couples or small groups. 928-204-2201. www.metaadventures.com

LUNCH

Just about anywhere in Sedona, you can find a place that is close by and serves tasty food. Makes me hungry just thinking about them! Here are a few faves.

The very best sandwich in Uptown (and maybe anywhere) is at **Sedona Memories**. Call in your order for a free cookie, but you may not have room for it with their huge sandwiches. 321 Jordan Road, 928-282-0032. The sandwiches are also delicious at **Canyon Ridge Deli**. Old Marketplace, 1350 W Hwy 89A, 928-204-4458. If you'd like to specialize, Sedona has many offerings. The lunches are light and go best with a glass of wine at **Wine Basket of Hillside**. Hillside Plaza on Hwy 179, 928-203-9411. The consistent local favorite for a very nice lunch is **Judi's**, which lets you sit inside or out. They offer excellent baby back ribs among many choices. 40 Soldier Pass Road, 928-282-4449.

You've got three extra-healthy choices at lunch. The healthiest sandwich or salad is likely to be found at **New Frontiers**, Sedona's biggest health food store. Old Marketplace Plaza, 1420 W. Hwy 89A, 928-282-6311. For healthy choices with table service, try the **Plaza Café** across the street. 1449 W. Hwy 89A, 928-203-9041. If you need your health food in take-out form, the lunch offerings are boxed and ready to go at **Rinzai's Market** in the Harkins Theatre Plaza. 2081 W. Hwy 89A, 928-204-2185.

For something economical, **Cafe and Salad Company** in the Safeway plaza is easy on the wallet. Safeway Plaza on W. Hwy 89A, 928-282-0299.

Three spots stand out for an elegant setting. It's high end down low by the creek at **L'Auberge de Sedona** resort. A splendid setting for people…and the ducks. Great quiche. Uptown, 301 L'Auberge Lane, 928-282-1661.

The best views are at **Tii Gavo at Enchantment Resort**. It's essential to call ahead, not just for reservations, but even to be allowed onto the property. Go for the balcony. Yummy black bean soup. 525 Boynton Canyon Road, 928-282-2900.

Great views close to town are at **Shugrue's Hillside Grill**. I recommend the Turkey Wrap, the Ginger Walnut Chicken Salad, or the special. Hillside Plaza on Hwy 179, 928-282-5300.

I've enjoyed the lunch specials at the **Junipine Cafe,** (1 mile north of Slide Rock State Park, 928-282-7406) and I've enjoyed an equally good sandwich at the deli at **Garland's Trading Post,** both located in Oak Creek Canyon. 3951 N. Hwy 89A, 928-282-7702.

In the Best-Lunch-Ever-Served-in-an-Outlet-Mall category, the winner is the **Marketplace Cafe** in the Village of Oak Creek. Prime Outlets, 6645 Hwy 179, 928-284-5478. Also nice in this part of town is the **Sedona Golf Resort,** with lovely views. 35 Ridge Trail Drive, 928-284-2093.

Tequila Lime Fajitas

Here's a sizzling recipe from a hot local chef, Martha Upson.

juice of 4 limes
4 cloves garlic, chopped
2 teaspoons olive oil
1/4 cup honey
2 teaspoons cumin
2 teaspoons paprika
2 ounces tequila (divided use)
salt and pepper to taste
1 1/2 lb. chicken, beef, or shrimp, sliced in strips or peeled and deveined
2 red onions, sliced
2 red peppers, sliced
2 yellow peppers, sliced
1 cup fresh cilantro, finely chopped
4 to 6 flour tortillas

Combine lime juice, garlic, olive oil, honey, cumin, paprika, one ounce of the tequila, salt, and pepper in a large glass or ceramic bowl. Add the chicken, beef, or shrimp and allow to marinate one to two hours. In a hot skillet, saute the meat quickly for two to three minutes, then add remaining ounce of tequila and the onions and peppers. Saute for another four to five minutes (until pink is gone from chicken, if you are using it). Remove from heat. Wrap the mixture in warm tortillas. Serve with pico de gallo and cheese if desired.

Fresh Lime Margaritas

With the rest of that bottle of tequila, why not make a margarita —always a tasty southwestern treat with or without a meal!

1 to 2 ounces tequila
juice of two limes (reserve 2 wedges)
1 ounce Triple Sec
2 cups ice
2 tablespoons kosher salt

Combine tequila, lime juice, Triple Sec, and ice in a strong blender and whirl to blend. Place the salt on a small plate. Run a wedge of lime along the rim of your glass and dip upside down in salt. Fill with your tasty cooling elixir and enjoy the afternoon. Cheers!

INSIDE INSIGHT

Making the Most of a Week in Sedona

Suppose you have a week in Sedona. Well, at least now we have a little time to work with! Let me congratulate you on the wise choice to hang around. Take the following advice and you'll see a Sedona that the two-hour tourists don't even know exists. Here are seven great days all planned out for you. Mix and match as you like.

First, spend a day on the trails. (Personally, I'd spend all seven days on the hiking trails.) Begin at New York Bagels & Donuts to pick up breakfast plus a sandwich for the trail. The three hikes listed under "Hiking" give you some options. Other good trails include Doe Mountain and nearby Fay Canyon. If you prefer bike trails, then consult the experts. Sedona Bike & Bean is best for novices, close to the Bell Rock Pathway. Mountain Bike Heaven is best if you want big thrills. Rent one of their high-end demos, join a group ride, and you'll come back with stories and a nickname.

Second, enjoy a day in Oak Creek Canyon. Stop at Garland's for food supplies and explore their outstanding Native American jewelry store one door down. Life in the canyon is also about Oak Creek, so you'll want to walk it or fish it. The West Fork Trail is historic, and

Slide Rock State Park scenic, and either can be complemented with lunch at Junipine Cafe at the resort. If you pick fishing instead, call Jim McInness of Gon' Fishen to guide you to the best fishing holes. You'll spend less time fishing but more time eating fish at Rainbow Trout Farm, which has grills to cook up what you harvest. At Indian Gardens, they sell juicy peaches in the summertime and hot cider in the autumn and winter.

Third, in one day you can see fascinating remains of ancient civilizations. Palatki hosts Indian ruins plus petroglyphs and pictographs, and enough rangers and volunteers to explain the difference. If you are staying in the Village of Oak Creek, stick with the southern the trio of glyphs at V—V ("V Bar V"), ruins at Montezuma Castle, and mysteries at Montezuma Well.

Fourth, moving from ancient art to modern, gallery hopping is well worth a day of your time. Take the "Sedona Art Walk" I've outlined under "Art." Stops should include galleries on the corridor beginning in Uptown and stretching below the "Roller-Coaster," i.e., the winding portion of 179 that finishes at Hillside Plaza.

Fifth, it's an interesting perspective to spend a day on Sedona's architecture. I suggest an eclectic mix of the religious, the retail, and the nouveau riche. Visit the Chapel of the Holy Cross for spiritual wonders, then head to Tlaquepaque to stroll among the porticos of an imitation Mexican town. Finish by driving up Jordan Road in Uptown to Jordan Park, where you can snoop around among the new homes on Sedona's priciest real estate.

Sixth, allow one day for Sedona's tour companies to show you what you might not find on your own. In fact, A Day in the West has just the right offer, not to mention the right name. They'll combine a jeep ride, a horseback ride, and a cowboy cookout for you. If you're sticking to jeeps alone, then try a deeper experience with Earth Wisdom Tours to explore Sedona's mystical side. See it all from above later with Red Rock Biplanes or Arizona Helicopter Adventures. You could also see it all from above earlier, in a dawn departure with Northern Light or Red Rock Balloon. Consult the "Land Tours" chapter for Sedona's best private guides.

Seventh, you now have the time to supplement Sedona with side trips. The Grand Canyon is two hours and 15 minutes away via the direct route, but there's an extended route that shows you much more. (*See the "Grand Canyon" essay for details.*) It's a full day experience. A half-day is all you'll need for Jerome, the ghost town west of Sedona. It's 35 minutes away and is worth visiting if you've got more than three days here. (*See "Jerome" for details.*)

Of course you're going to spend all seven days eating, but where? If you want to eat well but don't want to spend all the money on one meal, visit Sedona's "Little Italy." With 11 places serving some form of Italian cuisine on the west side of town, you'll have plenty of choices. A Pizza Heaven, Pizza Picazzo, and Troia's offer very good pasta and pizza at moderate prices in a nice atmosphere.

You know about Airport Mesa for the sunset: now try places like Red Rock Crossing, Snoopy Rock, and Lee Mountain. Insiders know that Sedona's sunsets are not best in the west, but to the east, where the setting sun turns the red rocks a glowing orange. Spend other evenings trying to find your own sunset spot. At night, remember to celebrate your good fortune. There's bound to be something happening this week at Casa Rincon.

Feel as if you need a vacation from your vacation? Finish restfully with a massage at Red Rock Healing Arts, and then listen to Jesse Kalu play the flute in a presentation at Sedona Pines Resort.

Here are the numbers you need: New York Bagels & Donuts, 1650 W. Hwy 89A, 928-204-1242; Doe Mountain and Fay Canyon are located on FR 152, left off Boynton Canyon Road; Sedona Bike & Bean, Village of Oak Creek, 6020 Hwy 179, 928-284-0210; Mountain Bike Heaven, West Sedona, 1695 W. Hwy 89A, 928-282-1312. Oak Creek Canyon begins north of Uptown. Garland's, Slide Rock, Junipine, and West Fork all follow between three and 11 miles along, on the left-hand side.

Jim McInness of Gon' Fishen is at 928-282-0788; Rainbow Trout Farm, 3500 N. Hwy 89A, 928-282-5799; Indian Gardens, 3951 N. Hwy 89A, 928-282-7702. Information on V—V, Montezuma Castle, Palatki, and Montezuma Well are listed in detail with "Indian Ruins."

To take the "Sedona Art Walk," see the "Art" listing.

The Chapel of the Holy Cross is at the end of Chapel Road, which intersects Hwy 179 approximately four miles south of the "Y" intersection with Hwy 89A. Tlaquepaque is just a half mile south of the "Y." Jordan Park is at the end of Jordan Road (in Uptown, take the left from the turning lane just beyond the first stoplight).

A Day in the West 252 N. Hwy 89A, 928-282-4320; Earth Wisdom, 293 N. Hwy 89A, 928-282-4714; Red Rock Biplanes, 928-204-5939, 888-866-7433; Arizona Helicopter Adventures, Sedona Airport, 928-282-0904, 800-282-5141; Northern Light, 928-282-2274, 800-230-6222; Red Rock Balloon, 800-258-3754. You'll find the directions to Grand Canyon in the "Grand Canyon" essay. To get to Jerome, take Hwy 89A west through Cottonwood, a 35-minute drive. See "Jerome" for what to do once you get there.

A Pizza Heaven, 2675 W. Hwy 89A, 928-282-0519; Pizza Picazzo, 1855 W. Hwy 89A, 928-282-4140; Troia's, 1885 W. Hwy 89A, 928-282-0123; Pietro's, 2445 W. Hwy 89A, 928-282-2525.

Red Rock Crossing is at Crescent Moon Ranch Park, at the end of Chavez Ranch Road. Take Upper Red Rock Loop Road off Hwy 89A on the west side to get there. Snoopy Rock is accessible via the Marg's Draw Trail off Hwy 179, a mile south of the "Y" off Sombart Lane; Lee Mountain is accessible via the Little Horse Trail off Hwy 179, five miles south of the "Y," or nearly two miles north of Bell Rock. Casa Rincon & Tapas Cantina, 2620 W. Hwy 89A, 928-282-4849; Red Rock Healing Arts, 251 Hwy 179, 928-203-9933; Sedona Pines Resort, 6701 W. Hwy 89A, 928-282-6640.

INSIDE INSIGHT

Making the Most of a Day in Sedona

Now, suppose you've got only a day in Sedona. You've got a lot to do today, so start early. Grab breakfast at the Coffee Pot Restaurant or get your coffee fix at Brew at the View. At either place, you are surrounded by locals and visitors who know what's going on and can give you more advice.

The smart visitor knows the best stuff in town is outdoors, so pick up some water and supplies as preparation for your adventure. Choose from Bell Rock Pathway for an easy hike, Brins Mesa for something moderate, or Bear Mountain for the extreme. (*See "Hikes" for details.*) If you need something even gentler, try Red Rock State Park. Instead, you could rest your feet and have the nature brought to you on a Pink Jeep Tour. I recommend "Broken Arrow," their signature outing.

Spend lunchtime in Uptown, taking time to stroll the promenade. Hungry? The best sandwiches here are at Sedona Memories Bakery Cafe. Insiders call ahead (928-282-0032) to avoid waiting in line, and to receive the free cookie with every phone order.

In the afternoon, head north to drive through the lovely Oak Creek Canyon, choosing Rainbow Trout Farm, Slide Rock State Park, or West Fork Trail to experience it at its best. As an alternative, visit the Chapel of the Holy Cross for fantastic views and spiritual uplift, then head to Tlaquepaque for some shopping. Head across the street if you'd like to have your fortune told at the Crystal Castle or the Center for the New Age. Wondering what a vortex is? You may not have time to figure it out, but you can try by visiting famous Bell Rock off Hwy 179 in the Village of Oak Creek.

Take note of the sunset hour (*see "Sunsets"*) and head up to Airport Mesa, stopping on top to see some views from the overlook. You can stay up here for some food at the Airport Restaurant as you watch the stars come up. Spend the last few minutes of your day making plans for a longer visit on your return!

Here are your numbers: Coffee Pot Restaurant, 2050 W. Hwy 89A, 928-282-6626; Ravenheart, 1370 W. Hwy 89A, 928-282-5777. Red Rock State Park is on Lower Red Rock Loop Road. Sedona Memories Bakery Cafe, 321 Jordan Road, 928-282-0032. Oak Creek Canyon begins north of Uptown on Hwy 89A. Rainbow Trout Farm, Slide Rock State Park, and West Fork/Call of the Canyon are two, seven, and 11 miles north on it, respectively. Pink Jeep Tours is on the south end of Uptown, 928-282-2137.

The Chapel of the Holy Cross is at the end of Chapel Road, four miles south on Hwy 179 from the "Y," or two miles north of Bell Rock. Tlaquepaque is a half mile south of the "Y," at 336 Hwy 179. Crystal Castle and Center for the New Age are across the street from Tlaquepaque. Airport Mesa is at the top of Airport Road, 1.1 miles west of the "Y" on Hwy 89A; Airport Restaurant is on the mesa, 928-282-3576.

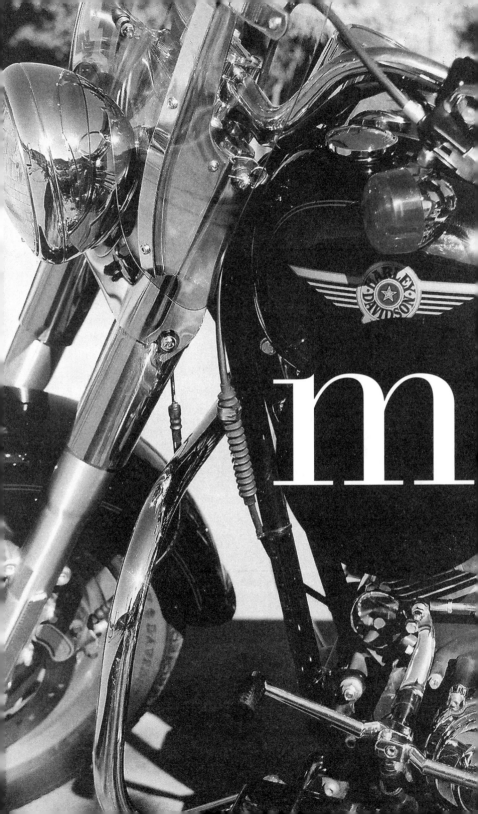

m

METAPHYSICAL/NEW AGE

WITH THE LARGEST NUMBER of metaphysical stores outside of California, Sedona has it all. If "New Age" is your bag, you're going to like it here. This is a difficult-to-define category. If you don't see what you're looking for, check the Alternative Health and Psychics listings in this book.

Crystal Magic stands out for crystals, although it has a good book selection. The store is nicely laid out, with singing bowls and an unexpectedly large amount of clothing. Jewelry and many gift items available. A big bulletin board with every possible New Age activity is outside. 2978 W .Hwy 89A, 928-282-1622. www.sedonacrystalmagic.com

Crystal Castle offers a wide selection of New Age products. Set in a building with high ceilings, it's a relaxing place to look for a book. There are plenty of crystal and gift items here too. Meanwhile, if you're looking for things to do, they've got the city's most massive bulletin board. 313 Hwy 179, 928-282-5910.

Books are the focus at Golden Word, which it does very well. They also offer a music listening center with 400 titles to choose from. Nice atmosphere. 3150 W. Hwy 89A, 928-282-2688.

The best thing about Center for the New Age is that, hey, it's a big place! If you've only visited teeny-weeny metaphysical stores with a psychic crammed in the corner, it's refreshing to breathe in the space. You can even walk out back, down by the creek. The Center has psychics, books, crystals, and gift items. 341 Hwy 179, 928-282-2085. www.sedonanewagecenter.com

Earth Mother Father Foundation includes a gift shop, healers, a pyramid and more. They offer ceremonies on the weekend and talks during the week, especially in high season. 2144 W. 89A, 928-204-1933. www.emff.org

Sedona Crystal Vortex has nice new owners who have created a positive atmosphere. Uptown, 271 N. Hwy 89A, 928-282-3543.

MOUNTAIN BIKING

THE ORIGINAL TITLE for this chapter was "Avoid Cycling, Try Mountain Biking." With narrow, shoulderless highways and drivers watching the red rocks rather than the road, cycling down the highway is not the thing to do here. The good news is that grippy red sandstone and miles of trails deep in the wilderness make this the best mountain biking this side of Moab. In fact, you might call it . . . mini-Moab.

If you haven't brought a bike, Sedona has several spots to equip you. Each offers rentals, usually by the half-day, full day, and longer. It's worth asking over the phone if dual suspension is available and if it costs more to rent a bike that has it.

Sedona Bike & Bean has distinguished itself with good service from well-informed employees. It is also the best choice if you want to start out easy—you can rent a bike and just cross the street to try out the Bell Rock Pathway. They feature a scale model of Sedona and its trails, allowing you to feel as if you were viewing Red Rock Country from above. Open 9am-5pm (Nov. 1 - Feb. 28), 8am-6pm (Mar. 1- Oct. 31) Village of Oak Creek, 6020 Hwy 179, 928-284-0210. www.bike-bean.com

Mountain Bike Heaven appeals to the hard-core crowd and is Sedona's oldest bike shop. These are the Kings of MTB Culture with their own line of videos, T-shirts, and coffee mugs. Group rides departing from here include a women's ride on Tuesdays; tough rides led by guys with names like "Wheelie Todd" depart mid-week and on weekends. Full-day 24-hour rental is $35 for a dual suspension, with high-end and demo bikes at higher prices. Open daily at 8am, but closing time varies between 5 and 6pm, depending on the season. Sun 8am-4pm. Daily, West Sedona, 1695 W. Hwy 89A. 928-282-1312. www.mountainbikeheaven.com

Absolute Bikes is a Flagstaff-based operation with a lot of experience that now has a shop in the Village of Oak Creek. Also close to the Bell Rock Pathway. 6101 Hwy 179, 928-284-1242. www.absolutebikes.net Mon-Fri 10am-7pm, Sat and Sun 9am-7pm. Front suspension bikes are $25/day, full suspension is $40.

Sedona Sports. Although the latter isn't a bike shop per se, their package deal may be the best in town. It includes a fanny pack with repair kit, maps, and a liter of water. Oh yes, and a bike, for a half day, all for $18. Mon-Sat 9am-6pm, Sun 9am-5pm. Across from Tlaquepaque, Creekside Plaza, 251 Hwy 179. 928-282-1317. www.sedonasports.com

The next question is where you should ride. **Bell Rock Pathway** is unbeatable for beginners, gentle and wide with interesting spots to stop at along the way. For a moderate route, consider the trails near Soldier's Pass or Deadman's Pass, which departs up the block from the Boynton Canyon trailhead. For expert advice, talk to the pros at the shops and get a map. Best available book: *Cosmic Ray's Mountain Bike Guide*. The cost? Less than the cost of getting lost.

Want a cool trail? Try a route I like to call "The Mystic Chicken." Begin at the trailhead of Broken Arrow, reached via Morgan Road, 1.5 miles south of the "Y" on Hwy 179. Follow the route toward Chicken Point, but head over to Submarine Rock if you've got time for fun on the red monolith. Beyond Chicken Point you connect with the Little Horse Trail, a fun ride that takes you through National Forest to a trailhead parking lot by Hwy 179. From there, follow the signs through the forest and then neighborhoods to reach the start of Mystic Trail, on Chapel Road. (You can make a short side trip to see the nearby Chapel of the Holy Cross.) Mystic Trail ends close enough to Morgan Road that you can find your way to it, but be careful of drivers watching the rocks, not the road. A great intermediate ride of five miles or so.

MOVIES

FEELING LIKE IT'S TIME to catch a flick? Sedona has two theaters, one with many screens and another with just one BIG one.

MOVIE THEATERS

Harkins Sedona 6 Luxury Cinemas. With six screens, you can expect current running films to be here in this nice movie house. Located in the plaza at the corner of 89A and Sunset Drive. 2081 W. Hwy 89A. 928-282-0222. www.harkinstheatres.com

SuperVue Theater lets you see an aerial view of Sedona without getting air sick. This IMAX theater plays a film about Sedona daily (great flick!) and whichever IMAX movie is around (Everest, volcanoes, sharks, etc.) serves as a second show. The ultimate rainy day option. At night they feature a current Hollywood hit. Seen on their enormous screen, it can be a real treat, but make sure you sit up high. Located just behind the Outlet Mall in the Village of Oak Creek. 6615 Hwy 179, 928-284-3214. http://supervue.com

VIDEO RENTALS

Prefer to stay in your room tonight? Video stores are well situated around town. On the west side there's **Red Rock Video** (Safeway Plaza, 2370 W. Hwy 89A. 928-282-5100) and **Inn House Video & Cybercafe** (Basha's Plaza, 162 Coffee Pot Drive. 282-7368), not to mention **Basha's and Safeway's** own video collections. In the Village of Oak Creek, try **It's Movie Time** (IGA/Weber's Plaza, 100 Verde Valley School Road, 928-284-5555).

Many of Hollywood's brightest stars have made Westerns in Sedona over the years. The list includes John Wayne, Henry Fonda, Yvonne deCarlo, and Jimmy Stewart. And believe it or not, even Elvis made a movie here. With Burgess Meredith in the supporting cast, it was called *Stay Away Joe*.

MUSIC

FROM COUNTRY-WESTERN to drumming circles under a full moon, Sedona's music reflects a creative multiple personality. Here are the best picks for who, what, and where to hear good tunes.

WHERE TO HEAR IT

The Highway Cafe deserves kudos for consistently supporting and promoting live entertainment. Rock & roll, karaoke, occasional jazz. 1405 W. Hwy 89A, 928-282-2300.

Casa Rincon & Tapas Cantina offers rock & roll, salsa (sometimes dance lessons), acoustic, New Age. Also the place for DJ Hareesh and DJ Arne, who pack the place. 2620 W. Hwy 89A. 928-282-4849.

Oak Creek Brewery Company shows off rock & roll, bluegrass, acoustic and New Age music. We're talking about the original brewery, not the one in Tlaquepaque. 2050 Yavapai Drive. 928-204-1300.

Old Marketplace. The patio in between Olive R' Twist, Sommelier de Sedona, and Ravenheart features live music on many nights. Various artists. 1370 W. Hwy 89A.

Rainbow's End Steakhouse & Saloon will remind you that it's not just "country," it's "sountry-western." 3235 W. Hwy 89A. 928-282-1593.

A number of restaurants will have an individual or pair of performers. These include **Shugrue's Hillside Grill** (Frost & Frost, 671 Hwy 179, 928-282-5300), **Javelina Cantina** (in the lounge, 671 Hwy 179, 928-203-9514), **Robert's Creekside Cafe & Grill** (guitarist Patrick Ki, among others, 251 Hwy 179, 928-282-3671) and **Savannah** (350 Jordan Road, 928-282-7959).

LOCAL SINGERS AND MUSICIANS

When they aren't on tour, you can see New Age specialist **Chris Spheeris,** guitarists **Stanley Jordan and Anthony Mazzela,** and dulcet-voiced **Vyktoria Pratt-Keating.** Without a doubt, **Sammy Davis** is Sedona's hardest-working entertainer: he and his band will not quit until you are singing or dancing.

Among true instrumentalists, there's **Ralf Illenberger**, an exceptional guitarist. No less adept is guitarist **Fitzhugh Jenkins**, who teams with percussionist **Eddie Baratini**, bass man **Troy Perkins**, and keyboardist **Zirque Bonner** to form **Bahia Brothers**, Sedona's best groove. Some of these same people perform with Full Circle.

If you want to get up and dance, **Limbs Akimbo** maybe the area's most fun band. I didn't think the boys in **Liquid Theory** were old enough to remember what "sca" is, but I like what they've come up with. See them now before they get famous and leave town. **Danny Rhodes and the Messengers** are a steady local presence.

Try to see singer Laurie Burke and guitarist/sitar-ist Bill Barns when joined by drummer Garrison Bailey to form **Belle Canto**.

For more mellow experiences, begin with **Jesse Kalu**, a marvelous flute player whose 1-hour performance is not just serene, it's spiritual. Jesse plays every weekend. You may hear **Patrick Ki** as you stroll through Tlaquepaque, and listen for Robin Miller, whose New Age music is the soundtrack for the red rocks. If you ask me, most destined for stardom is young **Michelle Branch**. The 18-year-old was nominated for a Grammy Award in the "Best New Artist" category.

CONCERTS AND EVENTS

Jazz on the Rocks is 2 decades young and is now well-established as the premiere musical event in town. Held at the Cultural Park on the third weekend in September. Look for the newly added Latin Jazz event in the spring. Office: 1487 W. Hwy 89A, 928-282-1985. www.sedonajazz.com

Verde Valley Music Festival has always been headlined by rock troubadour Jackson Browne, who could be counted upon to bring some well-known friends to this charity fundraiser for a local school. However, the early October concert was not held in 2002 and its future is uncertain. Check with the Verde Valley School for details. 928-284-1982.

Eco-Fest is a performing arts event promoting ecological education. The first one, in 2000, got off to a rocky start with great talent and crummy weather when torrential rains interrupted a line-up including B.B. King and Los Lobos in their inaugural year. They've stuck with it and made it a local institution. Look for this annual event in mid-September. For tickets and information, 800-594-8499. www.sedonae-cofest.com

Sedona Chamber Music Festival is held during the months of May and June. National and international soloists and groups. If chamber music is your bag, then check for the many other events this active Sedona society puts on throughout the year. **928-526-2256.** www.chambermusicsedona.org

When it's too hot down south, The **Phoenix Symphony Orchestra** comes north to perform at Sedona's Cultural Park. Check the Cultural Park's website for other events during the year too. **50 Cultural Park Place, 928-282-0747.** **www.sedonaculturalpark.com, www.phoenixsymphony.org**

RADIO

One thing is for certain: the good call letters were taken by the time Sedona got radio.

KQST, FM 102.9 "The Q" plays Top 40 hits.

KLOD, FM 100.1 "The Star" plays adult dontemporary.

KAZM, AM 780 has national and local news on the hour. It offers a music mix so eclectic that it borders on the schizophrenic: I once heard Barry Manilow, Pearl Jam, and Tony Bennett in the same half hour. If you lose your pet while you are here, they're the folks who will lead the search over the airwaves.

CD'S AVAILABLE IN SEDONA

The Red Rocks inspire both local and visiting musicians. Here are a few choices of the best made by either. Check **Crystal Magic, Crystal Castle, Golden Word** and **Sedona Books & Music** for the best music collections.

"The Spirit Room" by Michelle Branch, rising pop star.

"One in Spirit" by Jesse Kalu, and "Afternoon in Sedona" by Nicholas Gunn for New Age flute.

"Inspiration Point," by Brian Caldwell, might be called "New Age Techno" for its lyric-free synthesizer rhythms.

"Enchantment" by Chris Spheeris, for New Age synthesizer and guitar.

"Transcendence," by Robin Miller, is a local bestseller in the same category. "Lullabies" is a pretty set of songs to give your children sweet dreams, by singer Laurie Burke.

MOTORCYCLES

S EDONA IS A GREAT PLACE to feel the sun on your skin and the breeze through your hair. To rent a bike consider the following spots, all on Sedona's west side. Then cruise through the beautiful Oak Creek Canyon or head west up to Jerome for the big get-together at The Spirit Room. Substantial deposits (typically $1,500-$2,000) and motorcycle endorsement on your driver's license are usually required. Here they are in order of my recommendation.

RENTALS

Red Rock Motorcycle is the newest place in town renting 5 bikes from Dyna to Electric Glide, $95-$945 from 6 hours to a week. The 6-hour rental can only be done by walking into the store. 1350 W. Hwy 89A in the Old Marketplace. 928-204-0795, 888-200-HOGS. www.redrockharleyrentals.com

On many Sundays during the year, a group ride departs a 8am from the Harkins Theater Plaza in West Sedona, 2082 W. Hwy 89A. Check with the folks at Sedona Motorcycles for details.

Sedona Motorcycles has been in town the longest, and offers at least three motorcycles available for rent each day. Their rates range from $75 per day up to $120, depending on model. They typically have a Harley Sportster, SuperGlide and a FatBoy. Week-long rentals are as low as $525. Rentals include a helmet and riding leathers if sizes are available. 1195 W. Hwy 89A. 928-282-1093, 877-501-1325. www.sedonamotorcycles.com

Hemp & Hawg–Rent-A-Hawg is the rental specialist for Harley Davidsons, with prices around $175 per day. They've got gear for sale or for rent, from leather to hemp. 1575 W. Hwy 89A, 928-203-0346. www.sedonaharleyrentals.com

For repairs, consider **High Desert Cycle** at 2090 W Hwy 89A, 928-282-2255.

INSIDE INSIGHT

Photographing Sedona

More people take more photographs in Sedona than in any place in Arizona except Grand Canyon. Yet when they get home, the pictures sometimes don't do this place justice. Here are some tips to ensure that your pictures will measure up.

1. Shoot off-center. The simplest thing you can do to improve drab picture-taking is to move your camera so that the subject appears above, below, or to one side of the center point of the frame. Our eyes are conditioned to expect things to be in the center. When you move things over, it draws the viewer's attention and interest. In addition, it allows you to show more of the background of your scene, a nice option in this beautiful terrain.

2. Shoot with the sun behind you. Realize that there's a difference between natural light and reflected light. If this means sun in the eyes of your subjects, then count to three so that they can open their eyes for the photo. However, avoid blocking the sun and casting a shadow on your loved ones.

3. Fill your frame. See an object you want to shoot? Move or zoom in or out until you fill a substantial portion of the frame with it. But realize that sky, particularly deep blue sky with clouds, is also a subject worthy of inclusion.

4. Show scale. When shooting the big arch at Devil's Bridge, for example, have a friend stand on top. That way people will really understand its size. Want to show how tiny a certain wildflower is? Photograph it with your finger next to it.

5. Shoot during Magic Hour. In the hour after sunrise and the hour before sunset, nature's light takes on a vivid quality. Remember to shoot things that catch the sunlight, but not the sun itself. In Sedona, you'll notice that the red in the rocks picks up an orange glow, and the sky is a deeper blue. See the "Sunsets" chapter to understand specific times for your visit.

6. Stop standing around. Who needs another boring picture of two people standing up straight with an arm around each other? Nobody. Instead, get your friends to freeze while they're bending, leaning, stretching, jumping, reaching, or hugging. Posed, yes, but not looking posed. Smiling is an action, too!

Once you have the basics in mind, consider these advanced tips:

1. Tell a story. Take photos that will show the progression of your journey in Sedona. Shoot a sign that says "Sedona" on it, the name on the trailhead, or a calendar that shows the date. Along with the Red Rock scenery, show the car, jeep, or helicopter that got you to the spot. Then, to go with your outdoor shots during the day—how about an image from the night?

2. Focus on details. To balance your long-distance photos of the mountains, go in tight on small wildflowers, tiny rock images, and little rivulets of water in the stream.

3. Think in themes. If your shots were to become a photo essay, what would you like the message to be? The options in Sedona are infinite: water on the creek; plays of light and shadow; sunrise and sunset; tourists having fun; celebration; contemplation.

4. Shoot with personality. How will your photos be different than anyone else's? What do your photos reflect about you and your style? Ask yourself these questions as you begin and you'll find that you shoot more consciously. The results will express not just Sedona, but your unique view of it.

5. Shoot sideways. It's natural to take tall, vertical photos here. Make a point to take horizontal shots (called "landscape" format) of the Red Rocks though, and you'll be surprised at the difference.

6. Appreciate the animals. Even if you can't find a bear to pose for you, there are colorful creatures everywhere you look. You may not see the eagle today, but don't give up on that little frog. Photographing animals in Sedona conveys a sense of the living wilderness in ways that pictures of rocks may not. To see coyotes, javelinas, and the most colorful birds, get out there early...and stay late.

7. Know where to go when the sun sets. Why do locals look east, instead of west, when the sun is setting? We know that while the western sky is pretty, the juicy pics are found where the light catches the Red Rocks. For the very best sunset-photo-that-doesn't-include-a-sunset, head to Red Rock Crossing. From Uptown and the west side, take Upper Red Rock Loop Road to Chavez Ranch Road and follow it until you reach Crescent Moon Ranch. From the Village of Oak Creek, take Verde Valley School Road west off Hwy 179 directly to the parking lot above the creek. Alternatively, stay in the Chapel of the Holy Cross/Bell Rock area for great light as the sun goes down (and as it rises, too).

8. Keep only the best. Want a fast way to gain compliments for your photography? When you put together your collection after the trip, throw away any that aren't great! Instead of friends glazing over doubles of your average set of 36, they'll be wowed if you simply hand them your 10 best shots. It saves space in storage, too, and you'll find that your albums become more interesting to revisit.

See "Photography" to find out where to develop your shots, buy photo supplies, and have your portrait taken western style.

Happy shooting!

n

NIGHT LIFE

ALTHOUGH the town carpet is generally rolled up early around here, night owls are doing their best to change things. Going out is an enjoyable thing in Sedona, because everyone seems to be in a good mood. Visitors are happy because they're on vacation, and most locals are happy because, hey, they live here! Here are my picks for the most fun to be had once the sun goes down.

CLUBS, LOUNGES, BARS AND BREWERIES

Casa Rincon & Tapas Cantina pulls in both tourists and locals. The cantina has the best performance stage in town, although management isn't known for treating the talent well. Open mike night is usually Tuesday, when the quality ranges from ridiculous to outstanding. Salsa, and occasionally dance instruction with it, is offered on Wednesdays, or Thursdays, and there is usually a good band or D.J. on Friday and Saturday. (Look for Sammy Davis, the hardest working performer in town, and a guy who won't let you leave until you've had a good time.) There is usually a cover charge of $5 or less. A new troika of fun has emerged on W. Hwy 89A closer to the "Y," challenging Casa Rincon's past dominance. At the **Old Marketplace**, there are the smooth-as-silk martinis of every possible flavor at **Olive R' Twist**, Sedona's hippest bar. (The "Mollypolitan" or the "Espressotino" are insider picks.) Beware of smoke inside. Across the patio, a classy spot to be is now **Sommelier de Sedona**, which offers wine-tasting in a beautifully designed interior. The patio in between has a performance space, and the free live music makes this the scene when the weather is warm. It's much less uppity across the street at the **Highway Café**, a diner-restaurant with a fun bar where Tuesday night karaoke draws in a surprisingly big crowd. Often live music on other nights too, although the space is cramped. **Rainbow's End** is not just country, but "Country-Western." Bands perform in the best true dance hall in town on the far west end of Sedona.

Things are more relaxed at the **Oak Creek Brewery**, the best micro-brewery in Red Rock country. The popcorn is free and there is often entertainment without a cover charge. **Laughing Coyote** is pure working class, but often has the same bands that the tourists enjoyed the night before for a few bucks more across the avenue at **Casa Rincon**. **Javelina Cantina**, at Hillside Center, has a lounge which may squeeze a guitar player in one corner who tries in vain to attract the attention of the crowd away from the TV screens. No cover, good food, and a bit casual yet upscale crowd, if that's not a contradiction. **Canyon Breeze**, in Uptown, started off as a place for entertainment, but something must have gone wrong. Now you can get a drink, but if you want to hear music, you'll have to whistle. In Uptown I'd rather be across the street and down the block at **The Cowboy Club**. This is the hang-out for wedding parties staying at L'Auberge, tourists passing through, and Jeep tour drivers who need a tall drink of water. **Steak & Sticks** is the best place for billiards and is open later than others, and the preferred hang-out of cigar smokers. Located at Los Abrigados (on Hwy 179, 1/3 mile south of the "Y"), it generally draws in timeshare guests at Los Abrigados, and timeshare salesmen from town. Its neighbor **On The Rocks** splits the sports crowd with the newer **SkyBox** on the north end of Uptown. Both have several TVs and large screens. (Go Diamondbacks!) Newer in that neighborhood, **The Oak Creek Brewery & Grill** at Tlaquepaque is far more upscale than its brewery brother. Food and service are only adequate, but the beer and the digs are great. Too bad they can't decide on whether to keep the nightly entertainment or not. **PJ's Village Pub** has expanded, and now offers entertainment and food to go with all that somking and drinking. You'll find it in the Village of Oak Creek on West Cortez. **The Spirit Room**, located in Jerome, is a bit of a drive but helluva' good time if you ride in on your Harley Davidson. It's like the 60's all over again. Located in Jerome, about 30 minutes west of Sedona. On the west side look for the **Sundowner** if you just want to get drunk fast.

COMEDY

Maybe your most fun night in Sedona will be the one you spend watching the town's fabulous improv comedy troupe, **Laughs on the Rocks.** The group performs throughout Sedona, mostly on weekends at night clubs on the west side. They consistently come up with good, clean hilarity that pokes fun at the town's eccentricities. Don't miss it! Check with your innkeeper or concierge for their current performance schedule.

DANCING

Casa Rincon & Tapas Cantina. In front of the best performance stage in town is a pretty good dance floor. Live music or D.J. most nights of the week. Dark on Mon. 2620 W. Hwy 89A, 928-282-4849.

GAMBLING & BOWLING

Cliff Castle Casino in the town of Camp Verde offers gambling on the Yavapai-Apache National Reservation. Dragonfly Lounge nightclub has weekly entertainment, and each weeknight is appointed for comedy, karaoke, etc. Cosmic Bowling is their bowling alley, with fluorescent lighting at night. Head south 30 minutes to the casino exit off I-17. 928-567-7660.

STAR-GAZING

Take a drive up to **Airport Mesa** to watch the stars. There you'll see the stars above and the lights of the town below. To the west, you may notice what my friend Benny calls "Constellation Jerome," the lights source in the old ghost town on Mingus Mountain. You'll see even more stars if you head west and pull off the side of the road a couple of miles along Dry Creek Road. Here there is less ambient light from the town. Just be care-

ful of employees from Enchantment Resort speeding home.

LOCAL PERFORMERS

Sedona is full of talented local performers. Here are a few that play around town.

You might consider **Sammy Davis** and his group as the house band of Casa Rincon. They're lucky to have him: he entertains crowds every time. Other local musicians who frequently appear include New Age artist **Chris Spheeris**, guitar vituoso **Anthony Mazzela**, and dulcet-voiced **Vyktoria Pratt-Keating**. I've gifted my young nephew with the "Lullabies" CD from local **Laurie Burke**. **Patrick Ki** is a classical guitarist seen often

Expect a cool feeling at night in Sedona. Although January's high temperatures average 56 degrees during the day, the low drops to 29 degrees at night. July soars to 96 degrees during the day and dips to 63 degrees at night.

at Tlaquepaque serenading the shoppers. Multiple-personality musician **Robin Miller** can be found rocking out with his band, but has achieved more fame for his New Age keyboard music, which must be considered the background music of the red rocks. **Ralf Illenberger & Fitzhugh Jenkins** are two exceptional guitar players who I could listen to all night. Don't miss **William Eaton,** who doesn't just play beautiful guitars, he makes them. Young **Dave McGuinness** is an improving talent. **Jesse Kalu** is a marvelous flute player whose one hour performance is not just serene, it's spiritual. You can see Jesse on weekend nights at the Sedona Pines Resort and the Sedona Heart Center. When it comes to bands, the most entertaining groups in town include Limbs Akimbo, Liquid Theory, Combo Deluxe, Bahia Brothers, and Danny Rhodes and the Messengers.

NEW AGE GATHERINGS

There is an eclectic mix of full-moon drumming ceremonies, women's gatherings, and psychic circles that take place throughout the year. Here are a few consistent enough to mention.

On Sunday nights, Linda Shay hosts **Dolphin Movement and Meditation**, a 2-hour evening. Linda's positive energy guides this enjoyable gathering of the two kinds of people in the world: those who already love dolphins and those who will someday. Devi Yoga, 215 Coffee Pot Drive, on the west side. Check 928-204-0793 for updated schedule.

On Saturday evenings you can join the **Psychic Circle**, featuring Scottie Littlestar at Center for the New Age. 341 Hwy 179. 928-282-2085.

Suzanne McMillan's **Sedona Heart Center** currently hosts flute player Jesse Kalu on Friday and other events during the week. Located next to the Highway Cafe on W Hwy 89A. 928-282-2733.

Look for the drumming circle and other evening gatherings at **Earth Mother Father Foundation**. 2144 W. Hwy 89A. 928-204-1933.

PARKS & PASSES

MY NUMBER-ONE PIECE OF ADVICE for anyone coming to Sedona is always the same: get outside! The combination of stunning natural beauty and genuine accessibility make Red Rock Country the perfect place to explore the outdoors. However, discovering Sedona's wilderness has become surprisingly complicated. So before you lace up those boots for a hike, give this chapter a read. I'll list the places you can go, and the passes that are good to get you there.

THE LAYOUT

The chief reason for the complexity is that Sedona's public lands are maintained by several different agencies. First, there's the National Forest Service, which supervises the surrounding Coconino National Forest. Second, the Forest Service gets help from private contractors that operate certain fee areas within the forest. Third, there are several Arizona state parks, operating under an extremely different management system. Although there are no national parks or monuments in Sedona proper, there are several nearby, and these are handled by the National Park Service. Confused? It gets worse.

Most of the hiking you'll be doing involves the Coconino National Forest, and to park on it, you'll need the controversial Red Rock Pass. Also run by the Forest Service, and covered by the pass, are the wonderful ruins at Palatki. More on the pass below. Some of the most famous nature spots are operated by private contractors to the Forest Service. This includes places like West Fork and Crescent Moon Ranch, but here the pass is not valid. Even more well-known are a pair of Arizona state parks, such as Slide Rock and Red Rock State Park.

THE LOCATIONS

The **Coconino National Forest**. Home to nearly 100 great hiking trails, the forest accounts for most of the untouched greenery left in and around Sedona. Whether you hike back to Vultee Arch or just park by Bell Rock, you'll be on land administered by the National Forest Service, for which a Red Rock Pass is required. 928-282-4119. www.redrockcountry.org

West Fork/Call of the Canyon. Made famous by author Zane Grey, the gentle stream winds through a lovely canyon on one of the state's most historic trails. Within the Coconino Forest, this park is administered by a private contractor and charges a $5 entrance fee per vehicle. **North on Hwy 89A, 11 miles from Uptown.**

Crescent Moon Ranch. Home of Red Rock Crossing, this lovely park allows for a very gentle walk along Oak Creek, with a spectacular view of Cathedral Rock. Picnic areas are available here. As with West Fork, a contractor manages the park and charges a $5 fee. West on Hwy 89A for 4 miles, left at Upper Red Rock Loop Road. Down the hill, turn left onto Chavez Ranch Road and follow to just short of the dead end, staying on the pavement. **928-282-3257.**

Slide Rock State Park. The choice of Arizonans seeking to beat the heat for a century now. Located in Oak Creek Canyon, here the river has carved a chute through the red rocks that's ideal for slipping and sliding in the wet stuff. There's lots of history around here, where many of Sedona's first modern settlers lived. You'll find some of the first apple orchards they planted,

the fruits of which are sold at the Slide Rock Market within the park. Bring a bathing suit if you'd like to take a dip in the stream, which has cut a natural chute through the red rocks. An Arizona state park, also with an $8 per vehicle fee. **7 miles north on Hwy 89A from the "Y." 928-282-3034. www.pr.state.az.us/parkhtml/sliderock.html**

Red Rock State Park. Located on the west side of town, this park has a nice resource center with good information about local plant and animal life. The staff leads bird walks twice a week, plus other ranger-led instructional walks through the park's very gentle paths. They offer full-moon hikes, and you'll be amazed at how easy it is to see. Oak Creek crosses through this park too. For details, call the Interpretive Education Office at Red Rock State Park. Drive west on Hwy 89A for 5 miles to Lower Red Rock Loop Road. Follow this road until the park entrance on the right. **$6 per car, up to 4 people. 928-282-690. www.pr.state.az.us/parkhtml/redrock.html**

Grasshopper Point features a swimming hole (not open year round). It also provides beautiful foliage in the autumn. Allen's Bend Trail begins here. **$5 entry per car. North on Hwy 89A, look for it on the right, less than a mile beyond Midgely Bridge.**

Palatki Cultural Site. An excellent site for ruins and rock art. There's a visitor center here, and both rangers and volunteers ("Friends of the Forest," God bless 'em!) to help you interpret what you are seeing. Open daily, 9:30am-4pm. Take Hwy 89A nine miles southwest of Sedona to Forest Road 525. Follow signs north for 6 miles. Take Forest Road 795 for 1.5 miles to entrance gate.

Picnicking is also possible at a few other "Day Use" areas: Banjo Bill ($5 per car, $1 walk-in), Encinoso (Red Rock Pass required), and Halfway Picnic (Red Rock Pass required). All are in Oak Creek Canyon along N. Hwy 89A.

Honanki is only a few miles further, but the extremely rough road makes it seem like a long trip. There are ruins and rock art here, but no visitor's center. I recommend only 4-wheel drive vehicles (even better, rental 4-wheel drives) for Honanki. Take Hwy 89A southwest of Sedona to Forest Road 525. Open 10am-6pm daily.

V—V Cultural Site. Read it "V Bar V," the name of a ranch purchased and now on exhibit to the public. Personally, I consider it the best rock art site for many miles around. Note open times. Open Fri - Mon, 9:30am-4pm. From the "Y," take Hwy 179 and continue east under the overpass at I-17. Follow the signs east for 3 miles to the entrance gate. Passable dirt and gravel road.

There are no **national parks** in Sedona, but plenty within driving distance. East is Tuzigoot and south are Montezuma Castle and Montezuma Well. Read more about these in "Indian Ruins." Between here and the Grand Canyon are Walnut Canyon, Wupatki, and Sunset Crater.

"THE PASS"

In October 2000 the U.S. Forest Service began requiring the Red Rock Pass for parking on the national forests surrounding Sedona. The pass has caused considerable controversy, coming mainly from locals who don't appreciate rangers becoming meter maids. The Sedona City Council isn't fond of it either; it passed a resolution calling for the repeal of the program. The Forest Service contends that even if you only park at the side of Hwy 179 to take a photo, you need a Red Rock Pass. A One-Day Pass costs $5 (valid 1 calendar day); a Weekly Pass costs $15; the Annual Pass costs $20. The pass should be hung on your car's rear-view mirror. The pass covers all trails and even car pull-outs in the Coconino National Forest, Palatki, Honanki, and V—V. The list of what it doesn't cover is pretty long:

Not covered by The Pass:

• Campgrounds and certain day use areas including Banjo Bill, West Fork/Crescent Moon, Call O'The Canyon, Grasshopper Point. These are $5 per car, $1 per walk-in.
• Arizona state parks: Slide Rock, Red Rock State Park. These are $5 per car.
• National parks: Montezuma Castle, Montezuma Well, Tuzigoot. These are typically $5 per car, although Montezuma Well is free.

Dendrochronology—the process of tree ring dating—was invented by A. E. Douglas, an Arizona astronomer who studied ponderosa pine trees to find evidence that sunspot activity affects climate.

There are 5 visitor venters located at the north, south and west entry points into Sedona offering complete information.

South: Daily 8:30am-5pm daily, in the Village of Oak Creek in Tequa Plaza. 7000 Hwy 179, Suite 101. 928-284-5324.

West: Mon-Sat 8:30am-5pm, Sun 9am-3pm. W. Hwy 89A in West Sedona at the Sedona Cultural Park. Check the box office.

Uptown: Mon-Sat 8:30am-5pm, Sun 9am-3pm. Hwy 89A and Forest Road in Uptown Sedona in the Chamber of Commerce building. 928-282-7722.

North: Daily, 8:00am-5pm. N. 89A at the Oak Creek Vista Overlook at the top of Oak Creek Canyon.

Oak Creek Center: Daily, 8am-4:30pm daily, at Indian Gardens in Oak Creek Canyon. Fishing licenses and supplies available.

In addition, there are numerous vendors throughout town, from convenience stores to sporting goods shops. Your place of accommodation may also sell the pass.

PETS

IF YOU'RE BRINGING YOUR ANIMAL FRIENDS with you, here are some places that may come in handy. Policies with regard to area accommodations vary, so it is smart to call ahead. As for taking your pet into nature, keep two things in mind. First, regulations require that dogs be leashed. Second, teach them what a cactus is before they find out the hard way. Experienced pet owners also remind visitors that it gets mighty hot in Arizona. Leaving your animal alone in a car is not only unwise and potentially deadly, it's illegal.

VETERINARY HOSPITALS

What do you do if Fido has a problem in the middle of the night? In a town this small, you've got no guarantees. However, here are three numbers you can try.

Bell Rock Veterinary Clinic, 48 W. Cortez Drive, 928-284-2840.

Sedona Animal Clinic, 100 Posse Ground Road, 928-282-4133.

Oak Creek Small Animal Clinic, 3130 W Hwy 89A, 928-282-1195.

PET SHOPS

Jungle Hut Pets, 1590 W. Hwy 89A, 928-282-5615.

Sedona Pet Supply, Basha's Shopping Center, W. Hwy 89A, 928-203-9898.

Village Pet Supply, in the Village of Oak Creek. 90 Bell Rock Plaza, 928-284-5865.

BOARDING AND GROOMING

Make sure to book ahead!

Bark N' Purr Pet Care Center, 30 Finley Road, 928-282-4108.

PET PSYCHICS

Why should you be the only one who gets to talk to a Sedona psychic? Both of those listed here offer not only to communicate with your current pet but to help you get in touch with ones who have "crossed over."

Lynn McKenzie offers private session, workshops, and training. 928-203-9142, cell 416-219-3803. www.animalengergy.com

Intuitive **Ronni Hall** is the star of the TV pilot Animallinks and offers private sessions. 928-639-1126. sss.dogbunnytalk.com

PHOTOGRAPHY

JUST AS GREAT NATURAL LIGHT in Sedona ensures good photos, it also attracts good people to develop them for you. You'll find lots of folks whose love of photography led them to Red Rock Country, where they've opened a store of their own.

FILM SUPPLIES, DEVELOPING AND EQUIPMENT

Swift One Hour Photo Express is the winner of my informal poll of professional photographers, who consider it #1 for film developing. Daily, 9am-5pm. Uptown, 252 N. Hwy 89A, Suite 4A. 928-204-0069.

Rollie's Camera Shop seems to have been here as long as there has been an Uptown. If you need to buy a camera, this is the place. The "Tres Amigos" behind the counter know their stuff. Overnight developing. Daily, 8:30am-5:30pm. 297 W Hwy 89A, Uptown, 928-282-5721. www.rolliescamera.com

One Hour Photo Express is extra-friendly and helpful, at the "Y." Mon-Sat 9am-6pm, Sun 10am-5pm. 146 Hwy 179. 928-282-6606.

Maxi Photo offers 1-hour developing too, as well as a variety of professional services. Here's something special: for $150 they'll shoot whatever part of Sedona you want—from an airplane. Mon-Fri 9am-5:30pm, Sat 9am-4pm. Basha's Plaza, 164 Coffee Pot Drive, Suite M. 928-282-1107. www.maxiphoto-sedona.com

First Light Photo Lab in the Village of Oak Creek offers digital downloads and printing. 2-day turnaround. Call for directions. 928-284-5445. www.galleriaventures.-com

Walgreen's has staff with good photographic backgrounds. Plus they stay open later in case you must see that sunset shot you took developed. Daily, 8am-10pm. On the west side of town. 1995 W. Hwy 89A, across the street from the Arco station. 928-282-2528.

OLD WESTERN PHOTO PORTRAITS

Get gussied up to look like a cowboy, outlaw, or parlour girl, then have your photo taken. Sedona's **Wild West Focus** (333 W. Hwy 89A, 928-204-5530) and **Old Tyme Photo Works** (928-282-7802). Both are in Uptown and both provide the costumes.

PSYCHICS, INTUITIVES & CHANNELS

IF YOU EVER GO TO A PSYCHIC anywhere in the world, this should be the place. Like trying the wine in France or the pasta in Italy, it is simply the thing to do here. Let me first acknowledge that psychics and channels may be very different, but explaining how can be tricky. Trickier still is rating them for quality, which is often a matter of taste. Still, there are some tips that may help. First, get references. Ask as many people as you can around Sedona, and certain names will keep coming up. Second, don't assume that the best people in this field are at the best-known places. Those who can actually make a living at it succeed in establishing a private clientele and forego the high-rent offices on the tourist strip. Third and most important, trust your own intuition. Telephone the person to get a sense of who they are, and go with your best judgment.

INDIVIDUALS

Zeffi Kefala is a Greek woman who you will find both entertaining and astounding. A specialty is medical intuition. 928-204-0516. www.ancient-healing.org. Although it is her holistic manicures and pedicures that she advertises, people-in-the-know will tell you that **Deb Lovejoy** is one of the best intuitives in town. 928-282-7667, 928-300-9003. **Laurie Reddington** says she has had 8 near-death experiences and has received a gift with each one. (Does this mean she has 9 lives?) She is an empath and medical intuitive, and is strongly recommended by locals. 928-282-5159, 800-329-8991. **Claudia Coronado** transmits clear, helpful information. She offers tarot, past life and other readings. 928-300-2112, cell 928-300-2057.

INSTITUTIONS

Center for the New Age has the most psychics in town, by far. But the best? Clients often utilize the Center for shorter, cheaper psychic readings, but realize that it's hard to get to the root of an issue in 15 minutes or less.

The Center suffers terribly from turnover, making it hard to recommend specific people. The counter people can't help with a recommendation, as most of them arrived in town just moments before you!

A very reliable bet is **Jamie**, who offers aura photos and reading. **San Dan Yi**, a transported New Yorker, has two tremendous gifts: intuition and sarcasm. **Salena** offers both good readings and massages.

Meanwhile, beware the bearded man who greets you in the parking lot and asks your profession before deciding what to charge you. If you want to clean up your energy in a jiffy and for no charge, request a free Aura Cleansing. 341 Hwy 179, 928-282-2085. www.sedo-nanewagecenter.com

Sedona Psychics is basically the psychics over at Crystal Castle. Typically two psychics are working on any given day. Generally, the readings are of a good quality. 313 Hwy 179, 928-204-1535. www.crystal-castle.com

VORTEX TOURS

See "Vortex."

CRYSTALS

When it comes to crystals in Sedona, **Crystal Magic** is #1. First, the collection is impressive. Second, the placement and display of the crystals show that they care about their pieces. Third, they have their own mine in Arkansas. If only they would have passed on the savings! A professional in the business once said to me, "They

know what they've got, and they charge appropriately for it." 2978 W. Hwy 89A, 928-282-1622.

Spiritstone is a store that is small but packed with interesting pieces where you've got a better chance of bargaining. 122 Hwy 179. 928-204-2100.

Crystal Castle and its neighbor, **Center for the New Age**, can count on business because they are on the busy Hwy 179, and their collections are large enough that you can always find something interesting. However, their employees don't always know the crystals well. 313 and 341 Hwy 179, 928-282-5910.

Ramsey's Rocks & Minerals offers custom jewelry work as well as crystals for sale. It's managed by nice people and also close to the "Y." 152 Hwy 179. 928-204-2075.

Angels, Art & Crystals has lovely crystals…it's just the prices I'm not crazy about. They've moved next to Golden Word on W. Hwy 89A at the corner of Dry Creek Road. 2445 W. Hwy 89A. 928-282-7089.

REAL ESTATE, VACATION RENTALS & SENIOR LIVING

I F YOU FIND YOURSELF with a wonderful case of "Red Rock Fever," the truth is the only known cure is to stay. This chapter is designed to give you a few pointers on buying land, renting a place, or passing your golden years in Red Rock Country.

BUYING REAL ESTATE

1. "Location, location, location" holds true. You'll pay more in the Uptown and West Sedona areas, less in Oak Creek Canyon and the Village of Oak Creek.

2. Visit Sedona during more than one season. No matter how pretty this April day is, realize that it may snow in January or reach 99 degrees in July. Will your property flood in the monsoon season?

3. Avoid tunnel vision. It is easy to focus only on well-trafficked routes around Highways 89A and 179. However, if you spend some time driving into Sedona's nooks and crannies, you'll see land and homes that miss the spotlight.

4. A great deal of property in Sedona is sold to folks who never wind up moving in. They underestimate the heat or the drive time from Phoenix, or how different this community is from the one back home. Whatever the reason, you can save yourself a great deal of grief if you have a little patience. "Red Rock Fever" is a harmless phenomenon, but buying on impulse can be dangerous. (Note that every agent you talk to will disagree with you, and they'll tell you so. They'll tell you that a whole lot of other tourists will visit the property and snatch it away while you wait to decide.)

5. Subscribe to the daily *Red Rock News* (928-282-6888) or monthly *Red Rock Review* (928-282-0008) and talk to someone other than an agent about the town's major issues. Did you know about the state's plan to expand Hwy 179 to five lanes? That the city is installing sewers around town? That the pristine "Forest Service" land your lot backs up to could potentially be traded away to a developer?

6. Know your demographics. Every town in Arizona is under intense pressure to grow, and Sedona has nearly doubled in a little over a decade.

7. Real estate agents won't like to admit it, but there are plenty of FSBO (For Sale By Owner) properties. Check the *Red Rock News* or simply drive through town.

8. Your dollar goes a lot farther if you are willing to live in Sedona's neighboring communities. Cottonwood, Camp Verde, Cornville, Rimrock, and Lake Montezuma are dramatically less expensive. Heck, in some of these places you could buy a ranch for the cost of a small Sedona condo. The downside, of course, is that you're beyond the Red Rocks.

9. Statistics say that Sedona is the most economically segregated city in Arizona. In short, that means it is the rich and the poor around here. Most of the rich brought their money with them; the poor earn theirs doing service jobs in the tourism industry. Rather than focusing on a place to live in Sedona, you may need to first look at finding a high-paying job that will help you to afford it.

10. Know the market, or find someone who does. Do a CMA (Comparative Market Analysis) in the neighborhood you're interested in for going prices per foot or acre. Find somebody who knows the market. Ask "What are the top 5 lots in the price range I'm looking for?" If they can't answer, then they may be more familiar with a price range that won't suit you.

REAL ESTATE BROKERS

What Washington, D.C. is to lawyers, Sedona is to realtors. Chances are, anyone in this town who isn't a massage therapist, a psychic, or a jeep driver is a realtor, at least part-time. Having interviewed satisfied clients with personal experience with a number of brokers, I can tell you that you'll probably do well no matter where you turn in Sedona.

Standing slightly above a crowd of good brokers in town are the folks who helped me find my dream house, **Jim and Anne French** of **RE/MAX**. They were exceptionally helpful and patient and willing to go the extra step to make the deal work for me. Jim is one of the few people you'll find who actually grew up around here, and Anne knows precisely what's up for sale, where it is, and how long it's been there. **928-282-4166, 800-282-4166, cell 928-300-9654.**

A second recommendation is **Lee Congdon** of **Prudential Real Estate**. With her background in both science and the esoteric (she has a Ph.D. and has studied feng shui), you'll find that she has a rare combination of skills that will serve your needs. She has the intuition to understand her clients' needs, as well as the diligence to make sure they are met. 928-282-3737, 800-373-2912, cell 928-300-5050.

VACATION RENTALS

To really feel at home in the Red Rocks, why not stay . . . in a home? From cute cottages to golf course condos to expansive mansions, it seems like you can rent just about anything in town; this in spite of city codes preventing short-term rentals. You'll figure out rental agencies have gotten around this when you are quoted a "monthly rate" for a property you want only for a weekend. For cheaper but less reliable options, check the Red Rock News classified section.

J.B. Jochum & Associates may have the largest array of properties. 2155 W Hwy 89A, Suite 214. 928-282-5560, 800-249-6875. Check out properties on the web at www.jbjochum.com.

Foothills Property Management has offices both on the west side of town (1615 W. Hwy 89A, 928-282-9533) and in the Village of Oak Creek (56 W. Cortez Drive, 928-284-1112). 800-369-7368. www.foothillsrentals.com

Red Rock Realty posts a weekly rental sheet if you're in town. 560 Panorama Blvd, Sedona. 928-282-9199, 800-279-1945. www.redrockrealty.net

Sedona Rentals handles rentals with a minimum of 6 months, generally unfurnished. Basha's Plaza, 140 Coffee Pot Drive, 928-282-7109. www.sedonarentals.com

SENIOR LIVING

Sedona Winds (204 Jacks Canyon Road, 928-284-1021) and **Atria Kachina Point Assisted Living** (475 Jacks Canyon Road, 928-284-9077) are senior facilities offering various levels of service. To check them out, turn at the stoplight by the outlet mall in the Village of Oak Creek onto Jacks Canyon Road and follow one mile.

The area's housing is mostly comprised of single family residences with some condominium developments. Realtors reported the average home sale prices in 2002 in the $350,000-$400,000 range, but the diversity of housing in Sedona—from manufactured homes to mansions—makes averages less reliable.

INSIDE INSIGHT

How to Have a Romantic Weekend in Sedona

A substantial number of Sedonans come to Sedona to create or re-ignite l'amour in their lives. They've picked the right place. There's something about the feeling of Sedona that seems to make falling in love very easy around here.

This is where Sedona's B&Bs, cabins, and small inns really excel. Cozy and friendly, they let you be private when you want to be, and sociable when you choose. The Canyon Wren cabins are located up the Oak Creek Canyon, which makes them best in the warmer months, unless you like snow. Slide Rock State Park is nearby. The Inn on Oak Creek and the Wishing Well are best among B&Bs for romance. The former overlooks the creek, and rumors are the "Duck Pond" room gets the most "activity" among lovers. At the latter, you can stay in bed and have breakfast brought into your room, or take a hot tub under the stars at night.

If your loved one doesn't mind a very early start, then he or she can't fail to be impressed by a hot air balloon ride, complete with champagne breakfast. If leaving the ground is out, then see the chapters on land tours, horseback riding, and bicycling. An alternative is to rent a pair of Vespas on Jordan Road in Uptown.

If you're here on a weekday, stroll through Uptown if you'd like to do some shopping, and have lunch on the balcony of Canyon Breeze. To avoid the weekend crowds, try Tlaquepaque instead (south of the "Y" on Hwy 179). Nice for window-shopping, with pleasant arches, porticos and fountains to visit with your sweetheart. Have lunch at the Secret Garden Cafe.

Who can help but feel in love in Oak Creek Canyon? For a hike, try West Fork, which inspired the romantic novel by western writer Zane Grey. Or, for shorter a walk, try Slide Rock State Park. Even gentler—and closer to the heart of town—is Grasshopper Point, also on 89A. At any one of these sites, the creek flows musically, and walking paths stretch alongside. If it's winter and the canyon is chilly, there is gentle walking at Red Rock State Park, found via Lower Red Rock Loop Road, off W. Hwy 89A.

Prefer not to move much at all? Then have breakfast and be served in style by the creek at L'Auberge de Sedona.

Now everyone knows sunsets are romantic, but how can you see one where everyone else won't be? Take the rental car up Schnebly Hill Road. If you're in a passenger car, proceed just half a mile past the pavement. Here the road widens and you can park by the big boulders. If you've got some time and a 4-wheel drive, continue a few miles up to Merry-Go-Round, park, and walk out to the rim for spectacular views. Linger with your loved one just a bit after the sun is down. If there are any clouds in the sky, this is when they will catch the best color.

The all-time romantic sunset story reportedly belongs to rangers at Crescent Moon Ranch. Supposedly a couple came from the Midwest, saw the sunset here—and now live here in Sedona, tending to the park. Stroll by the creek here at Red Rock Crossing and watch the setting light on Cathedral Rock.

Rather than at sunset, wait until after dinner for a drive up to Airport Mesa. At night, the town glistens below you. Walk out to the dark observation platform (be careful of the barrier), look left, toward the west, and see what a buddy of mine calls "Constellation Jerome." The old mining town appears to be a set of stars in the sky.

For entertainment, there's fine wine at Sommelier de Sedona and tasty martinis at Olive R' Twist. Alternatively, flute player Jesse Kalu provides music that is just native-New Agey enough to put you into a romantic mood. Look for his one-hour evening performances in town.

Take it from a bachelor who has been around town: when the night really matters, go to René of Tlaquepaque. It is private and pleasant, and the food and service are excellent. Ask for the booth inside and to the left and begin with their very tall glass of champagne. Chef Walter's Chocolate Souffle dessert must be pre-ordered, so mention it when you call for reservations. Later, you can stroll through Tlaquepaque.

The atmosphere is more bubbly at Dahl & DiLuca, which offers all the traditional Italian aphrodisiacs in their outstanding cuisine. A corner table works well, but move closer if you want to hear the music. If romance means animal passions, and animal passions means meat-eating, then Savannah restaurant is best for steaks. Choose the table by the fireplace.

Even if you can't afford to stay at Enchantment Resort, you should be able to buy a drink there. If so, make reservations first, then head to Tii Gavo Grill and get a seat on the deck for a lovely view. Other guidebooks recommend coming to Boynton Canyon to see the sunset. Good thing you didn't buy the other guidebooks: the truth is that this narrow canyon gets dark early, and the sunset is impossible to see. However, you can get nice reflected sunlight on the cliffs if you are at Tii Gavo by late afternoon.

Flowers can be purchased at the Flower Peddler on the west side; pick up some chocolate truffles at Ravenheart coffee house on the way. Top Shelf Liquor on the west side, and Sedona Liquors below the "Y," can help you get that perfect bottle of champagne. To put it all in one basket, call on Gift Baskets of Sedona in the Basha's Shopping Center. You can pick all this up in style if you ride with Red Rock Limousine.

The romantic inns are the Canyon Wren Oak Creek Canyon near Slide Rock, 928-282-6900; The Inn on Oak Creek, 556 Hwy 179, 928-282-7896; the Wishing Well, 995 N. Hwy 89A, 928-282-4914.

Northern Light Balloon Expeditions is the oldest of the area companies. $145 per person. 928-282-2274, 800-230-6222, www.northernlightballoon.com. Red Rock Balloons offers a free video per reservation to help you remember your views from above. $155 per person. 800-258-3754, www.redrockballoons.com.

Vespa Sedona is located at 395 Jordan Road, 928-282-5690; Canyon Breeze is in Uptown, 300 N. Hwy 89A, 928-282-2112; Secret Garden is in Tlaquepaque, 336 Hwy 179, 928-203-9564. Oak Creek Canyon begins north of Uptown on Hwy 89A; West Fork is in Call of the Canyon Park, 11 miles north of Uptown; Slide Rock State Park is seven miles north of Uptown; Red Rock State Park, found via Lower Red Rock Loop Road off W. Hwy 89A.

L'Auberge de Sedona is technically in Uptown, but feels far away down by the creek. 301 L'Auberge Lane, 928-282-1661.

The turnoff for Schnebly Hill Road is two blocks south of the "Y," on Hwy 179.

To get to Crescent Moon Ranch, take Hwy 89A west, turning left at Upper Red Rock Loop Road, then following to the stop sign at Chavez Ranch Road. Turn left on Chavez, following around its curves to the park on the left side near the end of the street. It closes at 8pm sharp.

Airport Mesa is reached by driving 1.1 miles west from the "Y" on 89A. Turn left onto Airport Road and follow to the top.

Sommelier de Sedona is in the Old Marketplace Plaza, 1370 N. Hwy 89A, 928-204-9988. Olive R' Twist is across the patio, 928-282-1229. Jesse Kalu plays at Villas of Sedona (120 Kallof Place, 928-203-4320) and Sedona Pines Resort (6071 W. Hwy 89A, 928-282-6640) and now also at Sedona Heart Center, next to the Highway Cafe. René of Tlaquepaque is at 336 Hwy I-79, 928-282-9225. Dahl & DiLuca is at 2321 W. Hwy 89A, 928-282-5219. Savannah is at 350 Jordan Road, 928-282-7959.

Enchantment Resort is 525 Boynton Canyon Road, but don't expect to find any other addresses on the "block." 928-282-2900.

Find the Flower Peddler at 2155 W. Hwy 89A, 928-282-3994. Ravenheart is at the Old Marketplace, 1370 N. Hwy 89A, 928-282-5777. Top Shelf Liquor, 1730 W. Hwy 89A, 928-282-4476; Sedona Liquors, 122 Hwy 179, 928-282-7997. Gift Baskets of Sedona, Basha's Shopping Center, 164 W Hwy 89A, 928-282-7747.

Call Red Rock Limousine at 928-282-0175.

S

GALLERIES
SHOPS • DINING

SHOPPING

THERE ARE FOUR primary shopping areas in Sedona. Prime Outlets in the Village of Oak Creek has the highest density of brand-name stores including The Gap and Anne Klein. Hillside Galleries and Tlaquepaque are more upscale, located along Hwy 179 below the "Y." Uptown has the most shops selling Sedona and Southwestern-related souvenir items, although there are art galleries as well. I don't usually like to reveal my sources, but in the case of shopping, I'm happy to reveal my expert contact: Mom. She is a frequent visitor, and judging from the shopping bags, a major contributor to the local economy. Shopping in Sedona is definitely Southwestern, says Mom, who always appreciates the friendliness of local retailers and the overall quality of what is on sale. Price-wise, Tlaquepaque is the place for the nicest things, and Hillside will likewise cost—and offer—more. Uptown is less expensive with more trinkets. The west side of town and the Village of Oak Creek are good places to go to save a little money. Mom notes that most stores do not stay open late.

Here, with the input of Mom and many locals, is a list of Sedona's most interesting stores.

1 An excellent crystal collection and a good book selection is the formula for success at **Crystal Magic**. It is at 2978 W. Hwy 89A, 928-282-1622.

2 At **Environmental Realists** they feature handmade wood items, nice women's jewelry, and nifty little clocks. Tlaquepaque, 336 Hwy 179, 928-282-4945.

3 The fun never stops at **Flags, Kites & Fun**. But will the owner give you a ride in his yellow convertible? 202 Hwy 179, 928-282-4496.

4 World-renowned for Native American rugs is **Garland's Navajo Rugs**. Tremendous quality, although it may take you many moons to pay the price. 411 Hwy 179, 928-282-4070.

5 Top of the line in designer jewelry is **Geoffrey Roth Ltd.** But Geoffrey, did you have to put your new store where the entrance door used to be? Tlaquepaque, 336 Hwy 179, 928-282-7756.

6 **Gordon's** offers lots and lots of clocks and other unique items, at a wide range of prices. Hillside Plaza, 671 Hwy 179, 928-204-2069.

7 It's a long drive up Oak Creek Canyon for **Hoel's Indian Shop,** but it's worth it. Call ahead to make sure they will be open for you. Beautiful kachinas and other Native American crafts. 9589 N. Hwy 89A, 928-282-3925.

8 **Hummingbird House** in Sedona's historic Hart General Store is charming. On the corner of Brewer and Ranger, accessible from 89A or Hwy 179 close to the "Y.' Custom furniture, antiques, accessories. 100 Brewer Road, 928-282-0705.

9 For someting from the East on the west side of town, stop in at **Kokoro** in the Safeway Plaza. This Asian market and gift store has clothes, books, flags, and other items. All colorful, all exotic. 2370 W. Hwy 89A, 928-204-2742.

10 Cute resale stuff is available at **Ritzy Rags,** the town's best second-hand shop. 40 Soldier Pass Road, 928-282-1135.

11 You'll have the most fun shopping at **Robert Shields Design.** The performer/entrepreneur doesn't train his people to sell, but to put on a show. They do. Several stores, but the best is just below the "Y," at 181 Hwy 179, 928-204-2123.

12 How about something for the young ones? **Sedona Kid Company** has great games and toys. Uptown, by the Matterhorn Hotel, 333 N. Hwy 89A #8, 928-282-3571.

13 Take home some of Sedona's sunshine with a sun face from **Son Silver West.** Great chimneys, too, if you're driving. 1476 Hwy 179. 928-282-3580.

14 Find interesting women's fashions inspired by another era at **Victorian Cowgirl.** 204 Hwy 179, 928-203-9809.

It looks much older, but Tlaquepaque was built by Abe Miller in the 1970s, after a Mexican town of the same name near Guadalajara. The name (tah-lah-kah-pah-kee) is said to mean "best of everything."

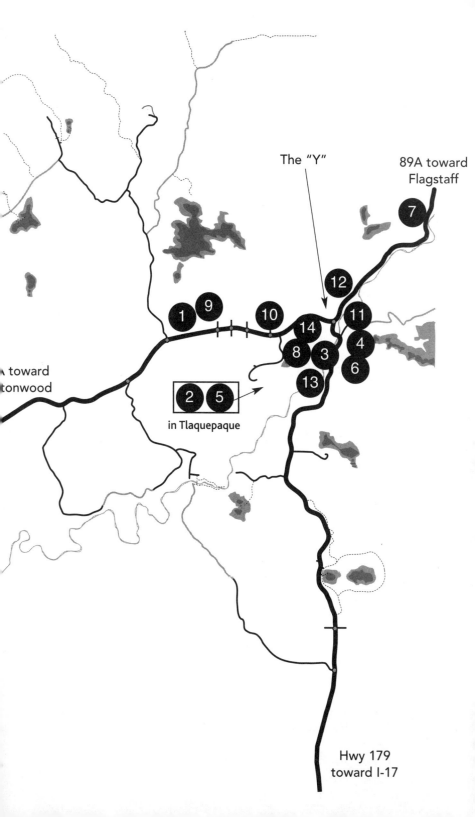

The "Y"

89A toward
Flagstaff

7

12

1   9

10

14

11

8   3   4

A toward
tonwood

13   6

2   5

in Tlaquepaque

Hwy 179
toward I-17

SHUTTLES, LIMOS & TAXIS

SHUTTLES TO PHOENIX AIRPORT

These van services pick you up at or return you to any terminal at Phoenix's Sky Harbor Airport.

Ace Express is the better choice if you desire door-to-door service. First, they schedule pick-up times around the initial booking. If you call early, there is a pretty good chance you'll get picked up in Sedona or at the airport relatively close to your ideal time. Some of their vans feature a few private seats and captain's chairs and tend to be less crowded. $47 per person one-way, $78 round-trip. Cash or check only. 928-649-2720.

Sedona-Phoenix Shuttle has regular runs and a large fleet. A stop by the driver in Camp Verde on the return trip slows things down a bit. A 2-hour drive by car is always 2.5 hours in this shuttle. Plan accordingly. $35 per person one-way, $60 round-trip. Pick-ups at Phoenix Sky Harbor at 10am, 11am, 12pm, 1pm, 2pm, 4pm, 6pm, and 8pm. From Sedona to the airport, departs at 6am, 7am, 8am, 9am, 10am, 12 noon, 2pm, and 4pm. Cash or traveler's check only. 928-282-2066, 800-448-7988 (toll-free only from Phoenix). Pick-up and drop-off are in the Village of Oak Creek at the Bell Rock Inn and at the Sedona Super 8. 2545 W. Hwy 89A.

LIMOUSINE SERVICE

Available for local weddings, or for a smoother ride to the airport.

Luxury Limousine is my recommendation when something smaller won't do, advertising itself as the area's least-expensive limousine and Town Car service. 918-204-0620. **Sedona Limousines** can also do the trick. 928-204-1383, 800-775-6739. **Sedona Airporter** offers a Town Car too. 928-301-4099.

CHARTER SERVICE

For trips around Sedona and in the region, contact Mark Avery at **First Class Tours**. 928-204-9416.

TAXIS

Bob's Taxi can get you around town safely in his big old jalopies. 928-282-1234. **Motengator** is the ultimate in old-time, small-town taxis.

BUS SERVICE

Greyhound runs bus service from Phoenix to a stop next to the Cliff Castle Casino in the town of Camp Verde, 30 minutes from Sedona. From points north, east, and west, Greyhound can get you as close to Sedona as Flagstaff, which is 50 minutes away. 800-231-2222. Locally, there is no public bus service to Sedona or within it.

SUNSETS

SUNSETS IN SEDONA are so special that I think it's worth discussing how, when and where to watch them. Watching sunset is an art form around here. It takes practice, but with a few Insider tips, you'll be a pro. First, realize that while desert dwellers in Phoenix and Tucson spend their time watching the sunset in the west, Sedonans look east. Why? Around here we realize that the most spectacular color will be found in the red rock reflections.

The most famous sunset-viewing spot in Sedona is Airport Mesa. The spot became better known when Arizona Senator John McCain held a press conference here, bringing his presidential bid to an end. If you're here at sunset, my advice is to hang around. Most visitors will leave as soon as the sun goes down. That's when the show is just beginning, especially if there are clouds in the sky. If there are, you'll see them pick up a variety of colors, from orange-red to lavendar, while the sky turns periwinkle blue.

Airport Mesa. West on Hwy 89A for 1.1 miles from the "Y," left onto Airport Road, then up to the top of the mesa. The pullout halfway up the hill is also scenic. Thinking strategically though, Airport Mesa is not an ideal spot for much of the year. When the sun sets to the extreme south or far north on the western horizon, much of the red rock will be cast in shadow early on. A broader eastern ridge stretches from the Twin Buttes behind the Chapel of the Holy Cross, along Lee Mountain, all the way down to Cathedral Rock and Bell Rock. Bell itself will be in shadow early, a full hour before the true sunset, so get there early if you want pictures. But perched on Bell looking out, you'll see genuine beauty almost every night. Follow Hwy 179.

Photographers have another favorite spot: **Red Rock Crossing**. The idyllic image is formed as Oak

Creek streams below majestic Cathedral Rock. Again, expect your best light (and best photos) to come 20-40 minutes earlier than the reported sunset. At this time Cathedral Rock is positively on fire, in a 10-minute burst of color that disappears quickly. West on Hwy 89A to Upper Red Rock Loop Road, left onto Chavez Ranch Road, staying on the pavement to Crescent Moon Ranch park. From the Village of Oak Creek, take Hwy 179 south to Verde Valley School Road, which turns to dirt. Follow to the parking lot 100 yards from the creek. If you're looking for a rugged getaway, take the car up **Schnebly Hill Road**. The road is rough and the view is west, rather than east, as I recommend. However, if there are clouds in the sky, you'll see the entire sky take on new colors during and after sunset. Take Schnebly Hill Road off Hwy 179, 1/3 mile south of the "Y."

SUNRISE

"What about the sunrise?" We've got good ones here as well, although they also don't come when anticipated. Because the sun takes longer to rise over the Mogollon Rim (pronounced Mu-gee-yon), it can easily arrive twenty to forty minutes later than the official time. In fact, for one

photo close to the rim, I waited nearly 90 minutes before sunlight touched the spot.

There are several wonderful sunrise scenes in town. You can try **Schnebly Hill**, whether via the rough dirt road or by hiking up the Munds Wagon Trail. The sun lights up the red ridges of the Schnebly Hill formation spectacularly. Or, head to the west side of town, driving on Dry Creek Road toward **Boynton Canyon**. There you'll see the hot air balloons afloat. Makes for a good photo if you've got a serious zoom. West on Hwy 89A for 3.2 miles from the "Y," turn left onto Dry Creek Road. A walk on the **Bell Rock Pathway** is perfect at this hour. However, rather than starting at the main trailhead by the Circle K, begin at Bell Rock itself, and walk north. Heading toward the "Little Horse" trailhead, you'll have the sunrise at your shoulder to the east and watch it touch Cathedral Rock to the west. If you're lucky, you'll see the hot air balloons rising to the northwest, at least 10 miles away. Take Hwy 179 south from the "Y" for 6 miles to Bell Rock. Another personal favorite is to stroll on the **Broken Arrow Trail**. Here, amid the setting for the Jimmy Stewart Western of the same name, you walk a mile as the trail rises to open sandstone plateaus. Catch it just right, and the high cliff walls will glow in the morning sunrise. You'll know once and for all: there's no place like Sedona. Take Hwy 179 south from the "Y" for approximately 2 miles, turning left onto Morgan Road. Follow the road all way into the trailhead parking.

OFFICIAL SUNRISE TIMES

January 1	7:35am
January 15	7:35am
February 1	7:26am
February 15	7:13am
March 1	6:57am
March 15	6:38am
April 1	6:14am
April 15	5:56am
May 1	5:37am
May 15	5:24am
June 1	5:15am
June 15	5:13am
July 1	5:17am
July 15	5:25am
August 1	5:37am
August 15	5:48am
September 1	6:00am
September 15	6:10am
October 1	6:22am
October 15	6:33am
November 1	6:48am
November 15	7:01am
December 1	7:17am
December 15	7:28am

OFFICIAL SUNSET TIMES

January 1	5:27pm
January 15	5:40pm
February 1	5:56pm
February 15	6:10pm
March 1	6:23pm
March 15	6:35pm
April 1	6:48pm
April 15	7:00pm
May 1	7:13pm
May 15	7:24pm
June 1	7:36pm
June 15	7:43pm
July 1	7:45pm
July 15	7:41pm
August 1	7:30pm
August 15	7:16pm
September 1	6:54pm
September 15	6:34pm
October 1	6:11pm
October 15	5:53pm
November 1	5:33pm
November 15	5:22pm
December 1	5:16pm
December 15	5:18pm

Remember, the official times are not typically when the sun will disappear. Assume a sunset at least 25 minutes early, in most cases.

INSIDE INSIGHT

Scenic Drives in Sedona

Whether you like your drives smooth or rough, Sedona's scenery can make taking one very enjoyable. At all stops along the way, you should signal clearly and slow down gradually to alert tourists following you who may be watching the scenery more closely than the road. How long your drive takes depends on how fast you drive and how often you stop, but plan a minimum of 90 minutes to complete any of them. Remember that no off-road driving is allowed in the Coconino National Forest.

SMOOTH ROUTES

1. **Highway 89A** qualifies as a scenic route from soon after the exit off Interstate I-17 on your way into town from Phoenix, and continuing through Uptown Sedona for a dozen miles through Oak Creek Canyon. So my first recommendation for a drive is to cover whichever portion of the route you didn't see on your way here.

For most people, that will mean Oak Creek Canyon. Little is required to improve this drive—simply follow it as it winds along the creek through both evergreen and deciduous trees that grow in the shadow of tall sandstone walls. Driving north from Uptown, head over Midgely Bridge and turn sharply left into the parking lot at the base of

Wilson Mountain. I recommend walking down below the lot and under the bridge to find a lookout point that offers a view above the creek. To get closer to the creek, you might stop less than a mile ahead on the right-hand side of 89A at Grasshopper Point. The windy road takes you down to the creekside, where the Allen's Bend Trail is a gentle half-mile that is easy to follow. The Rainbow Trout Farm is a bit ahead, also on the right-hand side. You can not only catch fish at the farm, but they've also got grills for you to cook them on.

It just gets better as you continue north on 89A, with stops such as Garland's, known for its wonderful Indian jewelry collection, and Slide Rock State Park. You can walk by the creek, take a dip yourself, or have some apple cider at Slide Rock Market. Continue on to the cafe at Junipine Resort to have a meal. Eleven miles from Uptown is West Fork, on the left-hand side of the road. This historic trail is a three-mile walk (one-way) made famous by writer Zane Grey. His book *Call of the Canyon* described the beauty of the autumn leaves in this side canyon. I recommend turning around soon after. Otherwise, you can continue up the switchbacks, climbing over 1,000 feet up to the Colorado Plateau.

2. In contrast to narrow Oak Creek Canyon, **Red Rock Loop Road** offers big, juicy views. Begin by turning onto the road off west Highway 89A, approximately 4.5 miles from the center of Sedona. There's a stoplight at the intersection, with the Film Institute and Cultural Park on the right. Turn left onto Upper Red Rock Loop Road, and you'll first pass Sedona Red Rock High School on the right. As the road begins its windy descent, you'll see a number of right-hand-side pullouts for picture taking. There's a stop sign at the corner of Chavez Ranch Road. I recommend turning here and following the windy

paved road a few minutes until you see the Crescent Moon Park entrance on the left. If you walk along the creek here, you'll come to Red Rock Crossing, with a view of Cathedral Rock in the distance. It is one of the prettiest spots you'll ever find.

Retrace the drive to the Loop Road, heading uphill if you want to return home. To continue on, turn left and don't worry about the change to dirt and gravel. It doesn't get too rough if you drive carefully. Eventually, after the road returns to pavement, you'll see the entrance to Red Rock State Park. It's a few dollars to enter, and your Red Rock Pass does not cover the entrance free. The park is home to numerous gentle trails and picnic spots, as well as a Visitor Center.

To finish this extended loop, turn left after exiting the park onto what is here called Lower Red Rock Loop, which will eventually return you to 89A. A right-hand turn onto 89A will bring you back to town.

ROUGH ROUTES

1. **Schnebly Hill Road** is centrally located, branching out from Highway 179 as it crosses the creek, a third of a mile below the "Y" intersection with Highway 89A. The road is not recommended for passenger cars, and you'll see why two miles ahead when it turns to rock. Last chance to turn around on the pavement is the Marg's Draw/ Huckaby Trailhead on the left, and there is a portable toilet here too. This road is little better today than in 1902 when Sedonans built it to bring their produce to market in Flagstaff, although it has now been somewhat graded.

One stop along the way is the giant red sandstone slab that serves as a parking lot for the Cow Pies Trail across the road. If instead you continue driving, the zigzag route continues to climb, and the view improves all the way. Another pullout comes at Merry-Go-Round, a red rock formation wrapped by a belt of pink-white sandstone known as the Fort Apache layer. If you've come this far, don't turn around before going a few hundred yards farther ahead, where Wilson Mountain becomes clear and northern views are revealed.

This is a good place to turn around, unless you want to continue another ten miles through the highland to eventually rejoin Interstate I-17. If so, head south on I-17 and take the exit for Sedona for a long loop.

2. Farther out of town is the trip to **Robber's Roost,** a cool route that few people know about. Drive 9.5 miles west from the center of Sedona on 89A and keep your eyes open for **Red Canyon Road,** labeled FR 525 by the Forest Service. Out here there are cattle drives up to the high country each summer. This is rough road, which you'll follow 2.8 miles before turning left onto 525C. Continue on 525C for 6.8 miles, watching for FR 9530 on the left.

You can follow FR 9530 for just over a mile to park by a seldom hiked trail, which drops down and then climbs up to this red rock formation. Stay to the left as the trail climbs the hill and you'll wind around the north face of the mound. Following along the narrow side of the mound, you'll eventually begin to see the cave where horse thieves once hung out. Here you'll find a rounded-out cave wall that is the stuff of postcards in town. Please respect this special spot and do no damage. From your parking spot, the hike takes under 15 minutes.

SUPPORT GROUPS

RIEND OF BILL? Visitors are very welcome to Alcoholics Anonymous. Call 928-646-9428 for details of the convenient meeting location and their frequent meeting times. Get information for narcotics, gambling, and other 12-step programs via the same number. Al-Anon too.

The **Cancer Support Group** meets at Sedona Red Rock Library. **3250 White Bear Rd., 928-282-7714.**

Desert Canyon Treatment Center specializes in addiction recovery programs. They offer month-long programs that draw on the assistance of outstanding facilitators from around Sedona. This is not a 12-step program: they offer alternative approaches instead. Shorter out-patient programs are also available. **105 Navajo Drive, 928-204-1122. www.desert-canyon.com**

Over the last few decades, the list of people choosing Sedona as a place to overcome substance abuse reads like a *Who's Who* of the entertainment world. People seem to think there is something special here that may assist those in recovery. Says one successful patient, "For me, recovery is not just about abstinence from drugs; it's about a renewal of self. Sedona opened my eyes up to that. I feel a connection with these red rocks that I think has held spiritual qualities for many people. The energy and appeal of Sedona itself made it easier to get in touch with more core, spiritual things."

SITOR
ENTER

BOX
OFFICE

→

t

THEATER

FOR A SMALL TOWN, Sedona has plenty of stage talent, and the odds are there will be some production going on during your visit. For current schedules, I recommend picking up the free *Red Rock Review* available around town.

Canyon Moon is the new name of the former Oak Creek Theatre Company, and they've got a new home as well. A cozy 100-seat theater has been constructed in the Old Marketplace Plaza, located on the north side of 89A on the west side of town. Main stage shows run through the year, but it's also worth checking out the "splinter series." These non-traditional events include poetry slams and storytelling but have little budget for promotion. 2003 shows include "Rosencrantz and Guildenstern are Dead" in March and "I Hate Hamlet" in April and May. 1370 W. Hwy 89A, Suite 6. 928-282-6212. www.oakcreektheatre.org

Shakespeare Sedona is the annual summer showing of the bard's works. When the sun goes down and things cool off, it's the perfect time to see a show. The plays are now held outdoors at the Sedona Cultural Park, or indoors across the street at Red Rock High School. The second part of Shakespeare Sedona is an excellent institute that teaches young actors in the classical tradition. The institute draws talented teachers from around the country. Both the performances and the classes run from mid-July through early August. 928-282-0747. www.shakespearesedona.com

If you think being in Sedona puts you in an elite crowd, you're not far off. Among the celebrities to have visited are Regis Philbin, Mel Gibson, Nicholas Cage, Burt Bacharach, Kelsey Grammer, Cher, Paul Simon, Cybil Shepherd, Stockard Channing, Meredith Baxter, Connie Seleca, and Brett Butler.

TIMESHARES & RETREAT HOMES

O KAY, MY PERSONAL ADVICE is to avoid them. No free steak or free stay-over is worth the pressure or, worse, signing into something for life that you may regret later. The irony here is that the high-pressure sales wouldn't even be needed—most of these places are actually really nice! If you're not interested, then beware of "Welcome Centers," "Tourist Information Posts," and "Movie History Museums," which are merely covers for sales points. If you are interested, then I've listed the locations of the best properties in town, so you can take a look for yourself. If you do want to buy in Sedona, then you might as well take advantage of whatever local deal they're offering in exchange for the sales pitch. They're willing to offer it to those who don't want to buy, so why should you get any less?

Fairfield Sedona has one property, the newest in town. Located by Pietro's restaurant. **2445 W. Hwy 89A, 928-203-9744.**

Sedona Pines is locally owned and operated, about 3 miles southwest of the edge of town. **6071 W. Hwy 89A, 928-282-6640.**

Sedona Vacations is the local name for ILX properties, which includes Los Abrigados Resort & Spa (behind Tlaquepaque), Los Abrigados Lodge (Uptown), and Bell Rock Inn & Suites (Village of Oak Creek). **928-282-2394.**

Sunterra Resorts owns the Ridge on Sedona Golf Resort (Village of Oak Creek), Villas at Poco (off Hwy 179), Villas of Sedona and

Sedona Springs (next to each other, behind Bank of America on W. Hwy 89A), and Sedona Summit (W. Hwy 89A, just before the Cultural Park). **Sales Office, 55 Sunridge Circle, 928-284-0689.**

RETREAT HOMES

Although I have no personal experience and so can't make a recommendation, I can mention two places in town to consider.

Dreamcatcher Cottage (928.203.0079) and **Your Heart's Home (928.204.2322)** can both be looked at on the web at **www.sedonasouladventures.com**

u/v

VEGETARIAN & VEGAN

RETURNING VISITORS will quickly realize that Sedona has lost a couple of its best vegetarian restaurants within the last few years. However, the slack has been picked up around town, and there are now very few places where a vegetarian can't find anything to eat at all.

EATING IN

Your major sources of healthy food in Sedona are **New Frontiers Natural Foods** (Old Marketplace, 1420 W. Hwy 89A, 928-282-6311) and **Rinzai's Market** (Harkins Theatre Plaza, 2081 W. Hwy 89A, 928-204-2185). The former has a cafe/deli and juice bar, and the latter prepares scrumptiously healthy veggie wraps, sunflower paté and other lunch-time treats for taking home.

EATING OUT

Tara Thai in the Village of Oak Creek (34 Bell Rock Plaza, 928-284-9167) is excellent, and **Thai Spices** (2986 W. Hwy 89A, 928-282-0599) on the west side is open to making adjustments. A number of places in the "fine dining" category will take good care of you. **René of Tlaquepaque** offers a Seitan Wellington that is delicious. They usually make 4 each night, so if you want to be certain they'll have one for you, order ahead.

Tlaquepaque, 336 Hwy 179, 928-282-9225. In Uptown, consider **Takashi** if you like Japanese food. Veggie Teppanyaki is suggested, and they can make tempura without eggs at your request. 465 Jordan Road, 928-282-2334. While we're discussing things left out, **Heartline Café** is by no means a health food restaurant, but they do make many of their soups without meat stock. 1610 W. Hwy 89A, 928-282-0785. For lunch, **Shugrue's Hillside Grill** offers both a Veggie Burger and a delicious Veggie Wrap. 671 Hwy 179, 928-282-5300. **Joey Bistro** (Los Abrigados, 160 Portal Lane, 928-204-5639) and **Robert's Creekside Cafe and Grill** (251 Hwy 179, 928-282-3671) have tasty, filling salads. In the Village of Oak Creek, consider **Pago's** for pizza and Italian cuisine. 6446 Hwy 179, 928-284-1939.

VORTEX

WHEN YOUR FRIENDS said "Stop in Sedona on your way to the Grand Canyon," you may not have realized the significance of their advice. Each year, tens of thousands have a strong physical or emotional reaction to being in Sedona (not to mention the millions that just seem happy to be here). Nearly everyone has their own explanation for it, and on some days nearly everyone around pretends to be a guide. The Insider sticks with those people and organizations who truly treat this as a full-time occupation. Use your best judgment when dealing with those that aren't listed here.

WHAT'S GOING ON HERE?

Each year, tens of thousands of visitors have a physical or emotional reaction to being in Sedona. In the overwhelming majority of cases, it's a positive feeling, ranging from a sense of peace to a smile on their face. That leads most visitors to assume it is Sedona's natural beauty that's putting them in a good mood. However, for a smaller number of people, what happens is more intense. Physical reactions include tingling, and emotionally there are those who are overwhelmed with tears. It can bring a joyful feeling, and a certain sense that you've come home. This isn't to say that the natural beauty of the area bears no role in this. It's just to point out that Sedona isn't just another pretty place. As with religious or mystical sites around the world, Sedona may be considered sacred ground.

Although we know that people have been coming through and feeling something unique here for a long *time, the term "vortex" (plural is vortices or vortexes) was coined by psychic/channel Page Bryant in 1980 and popularized by Dick Sutphen, who conducted workshops on psychic energy here in the 1980s here. Here are the people and organizations that can help you unravel the mystery.*

PRIVATE GUIDES

To get to know Sedona's magic better, I highly recommend touring with a private guide. Not just because I am one, but because your connection with Sedona may be an important personal experience.

Steve Benedict of **Touch the Earth Tours** is a former ranger, and so connected to nature that he sometimes seems more comfortable out in the wilderness than in his own home. A former trainer of the jeep drivers, he is known to clients as "Benny." He has a down-to-earth approach that is geared to helping you to feel the wonder of nature. 928-203-9132, www.earthtours.com

Sandra Cosentino of **Crossing Worlds Journeys** offers private tours focused on vortexes and medicine wheels as well as on extended journeys to the Hopi Mesas and elsewhere in the Northland. Good for shamanic work. 928-203-0024, www.crossing-worlds.com

Rahelio of **Sedona Mystic Tours** caters to the most esoteric crowd. It should be said that he is not Native American. He does, however, know much about Indian traditions and he offers some nice ceremonies. For a shaman-with-a-drum who looks the part, this is your man. 928-282-6735, www.rahe-lio.com

Last but not least is yours truly, **Dennis Andres** of **Meta Adventures**. My own approach is to take people into nature for a well-rounded journey that includes discussion of the geology, native history, and wildlife of the area. The focus, however, is to explain what's happening here in a balanced way and to give you the chance to feel, utilize, and decide about it for yourself. Also the best choice for those interested in deeper meditative work. 928-204-2201, www.metaadventures.com

GROUP TOURS

Suzanne McMillan McTavish is a long-time Sedona resident (around here that means more than 5 years) offering group outings. It's not easy to find guides with an office and an established center. Look for her at Vortex Tours next to the Highway Cafe. 1405 W. Hwy 89A, 928-282-2733. www.sedonaretreats.com

For less expensive group outings in a jeep, **Earth Wisdom** is your best choice for a soulful examination of Sedona's mysteries. Thoughtful guides attempt to explain the energy and refer to the Native American concept of the Medicine Wheel as well. 928-282-4714. www.sedonatraveler.com

BOOKS

If you have even the slightest interest in the subject, consider any of the following books.

What Is a Vortex? Sedona's Energy Sites: A Practical Guide is Sedona's best-selling book, written by yours truly. The book is divided into 3 parts, with a Q & A, maps and directions, and some options for deeper investigation. Widely distributed throughout town. 64 pages and full color photos inside, $8.95.
Sedona: Vortex 2000, by Richard Donnelly, long-time area resident. Available at all metaphysical book stores. A more esoteric approach, with numerous anecdotes included. 110 pages, $12.

Scientific Vortex Information, by Pete Sanders, includes a discussion of physics in his book. You can catch one of his free talks at the Sedona Spa at Los Abrigados. 64 pages, $9.95.

The Sedona Vortex Experience, by Gaia Lamb. 20 pages, $4.95.

WEATHER

THE GENERAL ANSWER to the question "Which is the best time to visit Sedona?" is "Any time you can." That's not just a Chamber of Commerce sales pitch: the weather here is truly pleasant for most of the year.

Spring and autumn are described in one simple word: perfect. Deep blue sky and comfortable temperatures are typical. Along with the nice weather, there's lots to see in the outdoors. Spring wildflowers abound in the high desert, and foliage is lovely in Oak Creek Canyon during the autumn. What about winter? Cooler temperatures prevail, but generally it is still comfortable to be outside. Daytime highs in the middle to high 50's and up are standard, but with bright sunshine and no humidity, it feels much warmer here than else-where. (Although it gets windy, "wind chill" is an unknown term around here.) With a sweater or jacket, it is another wonderful time to be outdoors, and there are far fewer tourists around. Winter nights, however, are downright cold, with temperatures dropping below freez-ing. In my experience, Sedona receives three to five snowstorms per winter, though the white stuff is typ-ically melted on city streets by noon. On the heights, however, it remains beautifully visible for days. If you're coming in March or April though, be aware of the annual "surprise" spring snowstorm. Curiously, it seems that we're just as likely to get a snowfall in early April as in early December.

An Arizona saying states that we have six seasons: "Autumn, Winter, Spring, Summer, Fire, and Rain." The two-part summer begins early, with June temperatures typically in the 80s and 90s and with no precipitation or humidity whatsoever. In July and August come the famous "monsoons," late afternoon rainfalls that pelt the red rocks. Often they don't come at all, but when they do, they are welcome. They cool down the temperatures, soak the dry forests, and are followed by amazing rainbows. If you're here in the summer, I'd advise that you do what locals do. Get up early to take advantage of cool mornings in the high desert. By the same token, you should note that the heat lingers late in the day. For outdoor activities, choose early morning over late afternoon.

AVERAGE TEMPERATURES

Below are the averages for dates throughout the year. Recognize, of course, that the last few years of weather have hardly seemed "average," with record high temperatures and drought in the area. Note also that elevation changes by more than a thousand feet between the entrance to Sedona at the Village of Oak Creek and the northern exit in the upper part of Oak Creek Canyon. That means temperatures at least five degrees cooler in the canyon than in the heart of Sedona, and at least two degrees warmer in the Village.

By the way, if you're checking ahead on the web before your visit, be suspicious. Most web sites report Phoenix, Cottonwood, or Flagstaff temperatures and label them "Sedona." Sedona is usually seven to ten degrees cooler than Phoenix and three to five degrees cooler than Cottonwood in the summer. By contrast, Sedona is typically twelve to fifteen degrees warmer than Flagstaff, although it is only twenty-eight miles away.

DAYTIME HIGHS/ NIGHTTIME LOWS

January 1	55/29
January 15	56/29
February 1	58/30
February 15	60/31
March 1	62/33
March 15	64/35
April 1	69/38
April 15	73/40
May 1	78/44
May 15	82/48
June 1	88/52
June 15	93/56
July 1	96/61
July 15	96/63
August 1	95/63
August 15	93/62
September 1	90/59
September 15	87/56
October 1	82/51
October 15	77/46
November 1	69/40
November 15	64/35
December 1	59/32
December 15	55/29

PRECIPITATION

"High desert" is a common phrase for the area's geology and climate. Technically, though, Sedona receives a bit too much precipitation to be considered a desert. Note that winter precipitation is as likely to come in the form of snowfall as rain, although we don't get much of either.

PRECIPITATION
(in inches)

January	2.10
February	2.16
March	2.47
April	1.16
May	.71
June	.26
July	.89
August	1.90
September	1.94
October	1.67
November	.38
December	.30

Average Annual Precipiation
15.94 inches

WEDDINGS

I F YOU'RE LOOKING for a place to tie the knot or renew your vows, the red rocks make a beautiful setting for your ceremony. To get a Saturday in spring or autumn, you should, of course, plan ahead. If you didn't, call the Sedona Wedding Hotline (928-282-6778) for help with your "getaway" wedding. The phone consultation is free.

LOCATIONS

The first bit of information is a disppointment—No, there are no weddings at the Chapel of the Holy Cross. Don't despair, there are plenty of other choices.

If you're starting small, and you'd like a church, begin at **The Chapel** at Tlaquepaque. I've always joked that this is the place where merchants come and pray to Our Lady of Retail when sales are down. In truth, it's a cute little place in the charming Tlaquepaque village that might be just right for you. It can be yours for around $250 and a deposit. A nice package option is to host your guests at René at Tlaquepaque restaurant afterwards. The nearby galleries provide nice spots for shooting photos. **336 Hwy 179, 928-282-4838. www.tlaq.com**

If you need a bigger building for the ceremony, the church at the **Verde Valley School** is quaint. **3511 Verde Valley School Road, 928-284-2272.**

For more than 100 people, go with The **Church of the Red Rocks,** which has glass on 3 sides and inspiring views. They're willing to work with people of any Christian denomination, but note that an advance consultation is required. **54 Bowstring Drive, 928-282-7963.**

Outdoor weddings are a nice touch, and **Red Rock Crossing** makes a famous backdrop. It costs $5 per carload to enter Crescent Moon Ranch park, or $5 to buy Red Rock Passes for guests coming in via Verde Valley School Road. This area features a view of dramatic Cathedral Rock, and the park attendants are helpful. **Bell Rock** is equally famous for weddings. It has some broad, flatter portions just above its base, if you think you can do a little walking with your wedding dress on. Don't count on the Forest Service to provide information. In fact, don't mention it to them at all. It's a "don't ask, don't tell" thing. **Located on Hwy 179 heading north past the Bell Rock Pathway Vista sign.**

Your indoor choices are basically the town's major resorts, and these will be more expensive.

Enchantment has a state of the art convention facility and a patio with a view. The downside is that they may not take your wedding if they think they can fill the date with corporate business. **5252 Boynton Canyon Road, 928-282-2900. www.enchantmentresort.com Radisson Poco Diablo** does a nice ceremony on their golf course. **1736 Hwy 179, 928-282-7333. www.radisson.com/sedonaaz Los Abrigados Resort** has a nice patch of lawn by the creek, good for both the wedding and a reception. **160 Portal Lane, 928-282-1777. www.losabrigados.com** The **Hilton Sedona Resort** is the other major option, and the restaurant gets good reviews. **90 Ridge Trail Drive, 928-284-4040. www.hiltonsedona.com**

MINISTERS/ CEREMONY FACILITATORS

Bob of **Sedona Weddings** is a minister who does a nice ceremony in a traditional Christian approach. If you include the doves, it's about $200 or so, although they offer video and other goodies in a larger package. If you'd like something in the Native American tradition, call **Uqualla**, a Havasupai Indian who gives a colorful ceremony for $300-$350 when he is not traveling around the world. **928-204-9757.** More "New Age" would be **Laurie Reddington** of Imagine Sedona. She is a psychic and healer who can also act as wedding coordinator. She prefers small weddings and works outdoors. **928-282-5159.** Rimpoche Za Choeje may be available for a Buddhist wedding blessing. Call his local contact Zeffi Kefala at 928282-6908, or check her website at www.ancienthealing.org

WEDDING PLANNERS AND CONSULTANTS

Bob and Sharon of **Sedona Weddings** add some nice touches, such as releasing white doves during the ceremony. They're better with smaller weddings. **928-284-1986, 800-551-0448.**

PHOTOGRAPHERS/ VIDEOGRAPHERS

Nora Stewart is the only photographer who shoots in large format. **928-284-3183.** For standard format go with **Dick Canby (928-282-2069)** or **Peggy Iileen,** who is friendly, experienced, and enthusiastic. **928-204-9522, www.brideand-joy.com.** Make sure to capture your ceremony on video. **Tony Sills** of Excellent Video is an experienced pro (he's done more than 800 weddings) whose prices are reasonable and whose quality is exceptional. Tony offers different tiers of editing and cameras, digital and multi-camera, for everything from budget to state of the art. Prices start at $200. **928-282-4624. www.sedonavideo.com**

FLORISTS

The Flower Peddler (2155 W. Hwy 89A, 928-284-3018), **Sedona Floral & Gifts** (3058 W. Hwy 89A, 928-282-3448), and **Mountain High** (2360 W. Hwy 89A, 928-203-4211) are Sedona's major flower shops, all located on the west side of town.

The Insider secret is that the woman at Basha's is as experienced as the folks at the florist shops, and the flowers cost less. **Basha's Shopping Center**, W. Hwy 89A, 928-282-5351. The problem, of course, is that these things change: the same was once true of Safeway, which employed a former florist shop owner.

TRANSPORTATION

Both **Luxury Limousine** (928-204-0620) and **Sedona Limousine** (928-204-1383, 800-775-6739) provide good service, but one wedded couple liked the latter's vehicle a little better. The **Sedona Trolley** is worth considering if you'd like some transport for your guests. They have up to 3 trolleys available to take your wedding party out to Enchantment, down to Bell Rock, or just about anywhere in between. 928-282-5400. www.sedona-trolley.com

TUXEDOS & DRESSES

Formal wear is available from **Sedona Tuxedo Rentals** at 928-282-7780. Consider **Victorian Cowgirl** for alternative wedding dresses. 204 Hwy 179, 928-203-9809. Twenty minutes away is **Cottonwood Bridal Shop & Dry Cleaners.** 148 S. Main St., Cottonwood. 928-634-3451.

CATERERS

The Heartline Cafe (928-928-282-0785) is very good, or try **Chef John Etlinger**, who makes delicious food according to our state's famous senator. The cafe's number is 928-282-0785. You can catch the busy chef on his cell at 928-360-1094.

OTHER NOTES

A **wedding license** can be picked up on the way into town. Simply leave I-17 at the Cottonwood/Camp Verde exit and turn left onto Hwy 260. Along the way is the county courthouse, open 9am-5pm, where with a driver's license and $50 you can get a marriage license. No blood test required. The Apple Orchard Inn can be rented out entirely or in part to host your wedding and your guests. 656 Jordan Road, 928-282-5328.

WILDLIFE

S EDONA has a remarkable diversity of animal life, and with a little extra effort you can see some of it. Many visitors fail to realize that the three-part terrain of high desert, riparian, and mountainous zones produce a unique group of wildlife. Here's a primer on locals animals.

MAMMALS

See that dog running across 89A early in the morning? It's not a dog. It's a coyote. They are in the canine family, but their coat tends to be gray to auburn in color, and they can be found individually or in packs if hunting. I can hear them howling at the moon in my backyard at night, and you may too. Stealthier and smaller is the Fox, which comes in red and sil-ver-colored species here. Keep your eyes low to the ground to see them.

One animal you're not likely to have back home is the Javelina, whose true name is the collared pecary. Looking a bit like a pig, and a bit like a boar, these critters are furry with a snout and reddish eyes and weigh up to 50 pounds. Always found in packs, they can't see for beans, but they sure can smell. Down in the same patches, look for the cute Desert Cottontails and big-eared, big-footed Jackrabbits. Smaller but only out at night is Arizona's state animal, the Ringtail. The animal is about two and a half feet long, but at least a foot of that is it's beauti-fully striped black and white tail.

Mule Deer have incredible ability to blend motionless into the scenery or to speed away in a high trot, literally leaping over brambles and cacti that hold their predators back. While not especially big as deer go, they do have enormous ears, which have led to their name.

The Mountain Lion is king of cats around here. Not much chance you'll see one of these, which will probably comfort most of you. However, the cats are out there in the back country, and I have seen their scat (droppings) myself. These are reclusive animals who will stay far away from any hiking trails. You've got a slightly better chance to see a Bobcat, a beautiful animal that's only the size of a col-lie but with very big paws for its size. If you're looking for foot-prints, remember that cat tracks will not reveal claw marks, unlike canines.

Speaking of paws, Black Bears are here in Sedona, generally far away from the crowds. An important exception is summertime, when they know there is food to be had at campgrounds in Oak Creek Canyon. If this means you, take precautions. Although a bear will retreat more often than not, you don't want to get in an argument with one over food. There are no Grizzly Bears in Sedona, and Elk can now be found only in the higher elevations toward Flagstaff, where they are plentiful.

REPTILES

For a better chance to see something wild, look down. Reptiles are colorful and available for entertainment. Lizards are common and there is no need to fear them. For example, you may notice lizards doing their push-ups while sunning on the rocks. A special treat is the Collared Lizard, which looks to be hand-painted in green with silver-white and black stripes around its neck. Look closely and you'll see the well-camouflaged Horned Toad, which looks like something out of the Pleistocine Era. If attacked, this reddish reptile can squirt blood out of its eyes. No kidding. Although this "toad" is actually a lizard, there are toads to know in Sedona, such as the Silver-backed Toad, which can be heard mating in the late spring by water spots.

What about snakes? It's true that Arizona has them, and Sedona is no exception, with the poisonous Mojave Green and Diamondback Rattlesnakes among them. The good news, if you are afraid of them, is that the odds are slim that you'll ever see a snake, and tiny that you'll see a venomous one. Even better news is that the odds of being bitten by one (assuming you don't try to pick one up) is less than the chance of being hit by lightning. They can sense our body heat from very far away and avoid the main trails. Remember too that since they are cold-blooded, they won't even be out until the weather gets hot. Nonetheless, if you want to make extra certain to avoid one, carry a walking stick to amplify the sound you make as you walk. Likewise, don't stray from the trail and avoid putting your hands into holes and crevices.

SPIDERS/INSECTS

As long as we're talking about critters that people get unnecessarily scared about, we might as well mention the Tarantula. To me, this is a spider with a black fur coat on, and if you can get over the conditioned fear, you may come to see what a truly beautiful creature it is. They are very gentle and are no danger to you. August—when they come out to look for mates—is the most likely time to see them.

You'll be pleased to find that Sedona is not buggy, and so is a wonderful place to be outdoors. The only place you'll find substantial mosquito life is near the creek or enduring water puddles. Ticks can be found in the tall forests to the north, but the lyme disease found through the northeastern U.S. is not present here in Arizona. More annoying but less harmful are the No-see-ums, aka cedar gnats, tiny little things that like to bite noses and ears. Avon Skin So Soft is said to repel them and is sold in quantities at Ace Hardware in the Village and elsewhere during No-see-um season.

TIPS ON SEEING WILDLIFE

1) Go out when the animals are most active. When it is hot in the middle of the day, they'll be relaxing in hiding. Choose early morning or early evening instead, when many of Sedona's animals are moving about.

2) Keep quiet.

3) Many animals can smell us long before they see us. Avoid perfumes and scented shampoos, which give your presence away.

4) Be patient, and allow plenty of time.

5) Appreciate those creatures that you do see. Don't take the lizards for granted, just because they are more visible.

6) Plants and trees grow vertically in nature, so I like to look for horizontal lines when scanning the wilderness to find animals. Look not for the deer, but for the deer ear, which will lead you to the animal.

7) You've heard it before, but it's still true. Brings lots of water.

8) Do no harm to any creature you see. If it frightens you, just back away and leave. Remember, you're a visitor in these guys' home. With the continual encroachment of development into their habitat, our animal populations are under stress and need all the TLC they can get.

Welcome to the land of Roadrunner and Coyote. You may see the latter in early mornings and late evenings and the former in the daytime in the Village of Oak Creek.

WINE

THE QUALITY OF WINE TASTING and wine making in Red Rock Country has made some big leaps with wonderful additions to town in the last few years. I can't think of a better place to sip some.

WINE TASTING

Sommelier de Sedona Wine Bar and Cellar has an excellent interior design that gives this place a nice European feel. The fact that it never seems crowded makes it a good place to try some excellent wines, though it probably doesn't make it a profitable business. A nice patio is available to relax outside. Old Marketplace Plaza, 1370 W. Hwy 89A, 928-204-9988. wwww.sommelierdesedona.com

The Wine Basket at Hillside is so pleasant that it feels as if a bit of the continent were tucked into Red Rock Country. Good not only for wine tasting, but also for splendid light lunches. The sampler platter is a favorite. Hillside Galleria, 671 W. Hwy 89A, 928-203-9411.

LIQUOR STORES

C-Market in Uptown carries wine and at least 30 imported and microbrew beers. Jordan Road & Hwy 89A, 928-282-4014.

Sedona Liquors is close to the "Y," at 122 Hwy 179, 928-282-7997.
Top Shelf Liquors is on the west side of town at 1730 W. Hwy 89A, 928-282-4476. They also have archery supplies. Should we be scared? **Basha's**, an Arizona-based grocery store, has an excellent wine selection, believe it or not. Hwy 89A & Coffee Pot Drive, 928-203-9504.

VINEYARDS

Brand new! A little bit of Eden in neighboring Cornville, where entrepreneur Jon Marcus has labored for years to finally produce a vintage at **Echo Canyon Winery**. At least a half decade in the making, several reds and whites are forthcoming. Available in select restaurants, as well as The Wine Basket. They have announced plans for tours in the future, so call to see what's up. 928-634-8122.

WORKSHOPS & RETREATS

THE NUMBER OF WORKSHOPS and retreats available in Sedona seems as large as there are hotels to host them and weeks to have them. Since hosts and topics change all the time, it's difficult to give a comprehensive list. Instead, I first list some of the sites and institutions in town where workshops happen on a frequent basis. Then I suggest the names of a few individuals who host events annually, to give you a taste of what is available here.

CENTERS

Sedona Creative Life Center is becoming the town's source for bringing in speakers on spiritual growth, hosting workshops in creativity, and highlighting music, dance, and theater performances. Call ahead to find out who will be in town when you are. 928-282-9300. 33 Schnebly Hill Road. www.sedonacreativelife.com.

7 Centers Yoga Arts offers 2-3 day yoga retreats in Red Rock country. Very intense. 1225 W. Hwy 89A, 928-203-4400. www.7centersyoga.com

Sedona Retreat Center might be accused of misnaming itself. It's closer to Cottonwood than Sedona, and given that it's off old Bill Gray Road (off Hwy 89A), it isn't really close to anything at all. However, the distance means they have had the space to create something very needed: lodging and dining facilities for up to 100 people. 928-634-5990, 800-875-2256. www.sedonamagogarden.org

INSTITUTES & ANNUAL RETREATS

The Sedona International Film Festival typically includes a workshop during its annual March run. See "Events" for details of the festival. Past topics have included cinematography and sound editing. 928-203-4849, 800-780-2787. www.sedonafilmfestival.com

Shakespeare Sedona is well known for summer performances, but fewer people realize that it also involves an institute to teach classical acting. The institute draws talented teachers from around the country to Verde Valley School from mid-July through early August. 928-282-0747. www.shakespearesedona.com

Is Sedona a nice place to do a workshop? Says one visitor: "I think the energy is so supportive of transformation. If people are wanting to do the work—and they bring that intention—the place will accelerate the process."

Red Rock Country. There are others, but in Sedona the fact that many events are not held on an annual basis makes predictability difficult. Check Four Corners magazine for more up-to-date information.

John Barnes, P.T., director of **Therapy on the Rocks,** conducts seminars in his myofascial healing techniques, typically in June and October. www.myofascialrelease.com

Tom Bird will help you write your first book and then show you how to get it published. He offers seminars and the "Intensive Writer's Workshop" here in Sedona at various times throughout the year. (Okay, I would think the apostrophe would be after the "s," but maybe I should take the workshop before I speak up.) 866-768-9847. www.ambassu.com for details.

ALTERNATIVE HEALING, EMOTIONAL RELEASE, SPIRITUAL GROWTH

I list here just a few of the many workshops conducted each year. A number of spiritual guides pass through Sedona, most often of the Eastern religion or New Age variety. Wayne Dyer, Ram Dass, Rimpoche Za Choeje, Sri Karunamayi, and many others have passed through

The Sedona Method is an emotional release process taught worldwide, but the big event in Sedona itself happens in October. (Are you beginning to understand why this is the busiest month around here?) Cost is approximately $800 for 1 week, not including room and board. **888-282-5656.** www.sedonamethod.com

Scott Walker instructs the N.E.T. process, also designed for physical and emotional relief, at Poco Diablo resort in October or November. www.netmindbody.com

Beth Rigby brings her "Global Dance" program for inspiration and movement in the spring and fall each year in Sedona. The retreat usually involves meditation and other spiritual activities. www.bethrigby.com

WORSHIP

I N SUCH A SPIRITUAL PLACE, you'd naturally expect all faiths to be well represented. Below are the addresses and times of weekend services when available. For Buddhist ceremonies, Satsangs, and other ceremonies of Asian-based faiths, inquire at New Age shops in town for details. Finally, a chapter for which I don't need to make a recommendation.

Sedona First Assembly of God, 150 Dry Creek Road. 928-282-7463.

West Sedona Baptist Church, 120 Deer Trail Drive, 928282-7478.

Crestview Community Church (Southern Baptist), 1090 W. Hwy 89A, 928-282-7405.

Village Park Baptist Church, 55 Canyon Diablo Drive, 928-284-3000.

The Master's Bible Church, 175 Kallof Place, 928-282-2155.

St. John Vianney (Catholic), (Sat 5:30pm, Sun 8am & 10:30am; Spanish Mass 6pm). Located at 180 Soldier Pass Road. 928-282-7545. The Catholic parish runs the Chapel of the Holy Cross but you won't find any services there. It is open to visit every day except Thanksgiving, Christmas, and Easter, from 9am-5pm. 780 Chapel Road. Nice gift shop.

Solid Rock Church of Sedona (Charismatic/Word), 2301 W. Hwy 89A, Suite 101, 928-203-4900.

First Church of Christ Scientist, (10:30am), 928-2823810.

Church of Christ, 2757 W. Hwy 89A, 928-282-7707. If no answer, call 928-203-0356.

Church of Jesus Christ of Latter Day Saints, Sedona Ward, 160 Mormon Hill Road, 928-282-3555.

Church of the Red Rocks Congregational UCC (8:30 and 10:30am), 54 Bowstring Drive, 928-282-7963.

VOC Community Church of the Nazarene, 55 Rojo Drive, 928-284-0015.

Wayside Chapel Sedona Community Church (Nondenominational). An Uptown landmark at 401 N. Hwy 89A, 928-282-4262.

Diocese of the Blessed Sacrament (Episcopal), 928-204-2599.

St. Andrew's Episcopal Church (8 & 10am, summer 9am), 100 Arroyo Pinon Drive, 928-282-4457.

St. Luke's Episcopal Church (8 & 10am), Hwy 179 & Meadowlark Road, 928-282-7366.

Jewish Community of Sedona is raising money for a synagogue. In the meantime, call 928-204-1286.

Christ Lutheran Church of Sedona (8:30 & 10:30am), 25 Chapel Road, 928-282-1022.

Rock of Ages Lutheran Church, 390 Dry Creek Road, 928-282-4091.

Sedona United Methodist Church, 3026 S. Hwy 179, 928-282-1780.

Church of the Golden Age (New Age), 164 Coffee Pot Drive, 928-282-3856.

Crystal Sanctuary of the Western Catholic Church of Malabar (New Age), 40 Goodrow Lane.

Rainbow Ray Focus (Non-denominational), 225 Airport Road, 928-282-3427.

Sedona Seventh-Day Adventist Church, 680 Sunset Drive, 928-282-5121.

Unitarian Universalist Fellowship, 45 Blue Canyon Circle, 928-284-9862.

Unity Church of Sedona, 65 Deer Trail, 928-282-7181.

Christ Center Wesleyan Church, 580 Brewer Road, 928-282-9767.

Consider a trip to the Chapel of the Holy Cross, Sedona's most inspired building. The local parish puts it this way: "Visitors who expect to find the Chapel as just another charming site are often surprised to find themselves deeply moved by the powerful spirituality emanating from this simple building and its location among Sedona's red rocks." The commonly held notion is that the Chapel was designed by America's architectural icon Frank Lloyd Wright, but in fact it was his son, Lloyd Wright, who helped create the original plans.

YOGA

W ELCOME TO YOGA HEAVEN. You could practically trip into a good yoga studio in Sedona, there are so many. Great if you are away from home where you normally do yoga, and even better if you are a beginner wanting to give it a shot. Here are the best places to drop in for a class during your visit, or to find out about yoga-focused retreats.

YOGA STUDIOS

If **7 Centers Yoga Arts** were a laboratory, then owners Gary and Ruth would be the chief scientists. Incredibly dedicated and disciplined, they and other instructors offer classes in a couple of styles, with standard Hatha and Tibetan as specialties. The Kundalini class with Gary is exceptional and rigorous. The periodic "Dance Your Wild Child" sessions with Lin Hunting are based on Gabrielle Roth's work in dance. Great fun, no training or experience required. Yoga teacher training also offered a couple of times a year. 1225 W. Hwy 89A, 928-203-4400. www.7centersyoga.com

Devi Yoga focuses on Ashtanga Yoga, a more vigorous style than Hatha and a great workout. Although Ashtanga (sometimes called "power yoga" or "astanga") has its share of hard-core types, it is instead taught gently and compassionately here by the studio's positive owner, Soni, and her brothers. These people are so beautiful it's almost worth going just to stare at them. 215 Coffee Pot Drive, 928-203-4046. www.deviyoga.com

Bikram Yoga College of Yoga is on the corner of Southwest Drive, one block in from Hwy 89A. Bikram is an intense workout, not for the faint-hearted. Lynda Weiss is the director. 2855 Southwest Drive, 928-203 9642.

Finally, yoga is often taught at local health clubs, such as Sedona Spa (at Los Abrigados Resort), Mii Ama Spa, Enchantment Resort, Sedona Racquet Club, and Sedona Golf Resort (the health club at the Hilton, known to locals as "The Ridge"). Drop-in rates are sometimes available.

INDIVIDUAL INSTRUCTORS

Sedona has a number of outstanding individuals who instruct but who may or may not have their own studios. When trying to discern between those who are here to stay and those who pass on through, these are the instructors I turn to. By the way, almost everyone has taken another name, so don't be alarmed if it is "Shanti," "Shakti," or "Shakira" that answers when you call ahead.

Garielle now has her own nice studio where she offers Hatha yoga, postures, breathing, relaxation, meditation, private study, and back exercises. All levels. **80 Willow Drive, 928-282-5839.**

Johanna Mosca (Maheshvari) is a very knowledgeable instructor and author who offers "Yoga Hikes" and Phoenix Rising yoga therapy. Her book is called "Yoga Life: 10 Steps to Freedom." This is a powerful approach to dealing with personal blockages, perhaps better categorized as healing instead of exercise. **928-282-9592. www.sedonaspirityoga.com**

South African **Tania Block** has made a beautiful yoga video called "The Spirit of Yoga in Sedona." She's usually found teaching Hatha yoga in the Village of Oak Creek. **928-284-5153. www.beeunlimited.com**

YOGA RETREATS

7 Centers offers workshops at various times throughout the year, including teacher training. Best word to describe them? "Intense." Johanna Mosca offers weekend getaways and 6-day intensive retreats. Finally, keep your eyes open for the many out-of-towners who come to host workshops here.

Best month you might have considered coming but you shouldn't: June. It's hot from beginning to end and bone dry. If you have no other choice, at least try to spend your time in cooler Oak Creek Canyon. Best month you might not have considered but you should: November. Less crowded than October and the weather and foliage are marvelous.

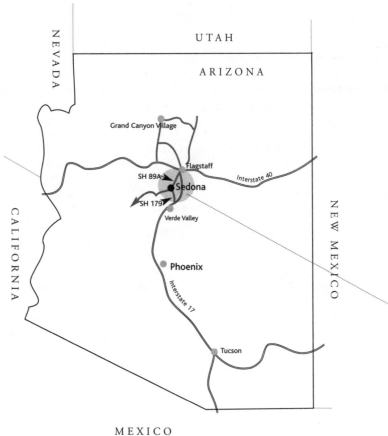

DRIVING DISTANCES

From Sedona	Miles	Approximate driving time
To Flagstaff, AZ	28	50 minutes
To Grand Canyon National Park	117	2 hours, 15 minutes
To Phoenix, AZ	118	2 hours
To Las Vegas, NV	279	5 hours
To San Diego, CA	466	7 to 8 hours
To Los Angeles, CA	483	8 to 9 hours
To Denver, CO	860	13 hours

DRIVING DISTANCES

Around Sedona	Miles	Approximate driving time
Uptown to West Sedona	2	3 minutes
Uptown to Oak Creek Canyon	5-12	10-25 minutes
Village of Oak Creek to Uptown	8	15 minutes
Village of Oak Creek to West Sedona	10	18 minutes
Uptown to Jerome	26	35 minutes
Village of Oak Creek to Oak Creek Canyon	10	25 minutes
Uptown to Interstate 17	15	23 minutes

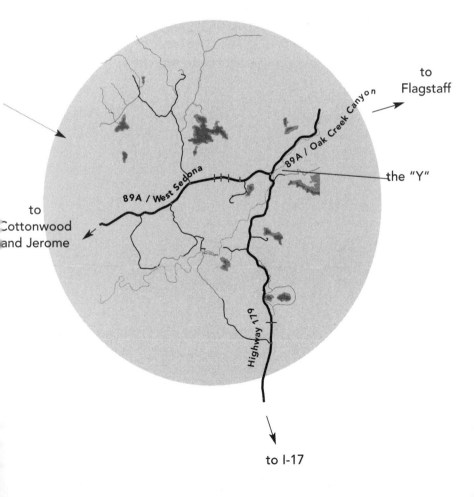

INDEX

To order this book:

For all orders in states outside of AZ, send $23.00 (which includes shipping/handling). For all orders within AZ, send $24.70 (which also includes sales tax). Mail to:

Dreams In Action Distribution

P.O. Box 1894, Dept. IG-B

Sedona, AZ 86339

Please include your name, mailing address and phone number/e-mail address (this is for order processing purposes only) with your order.

We invite you to visit our web site: **dreamsinaction.us**

Special note to corporations, businesses and professional organizations: Quantity discounts are available on bulk purchases of the book for educational, premium, or gift purposes. Please contact Dreams In Action Distribution at (928) 204-1560 or e-mail us at **info@dreamsinaction.us**.